ジブリ文庫

# GHIBLIOTHEQUE

# AUTHORS' ACKNOWLEDGEMENTS

Ghibliotheque and this book were the result of a lot of hard work and support from a lot more people than just Michael and Jake. Much like with Studio Ghibli itself, there are many behind the scenes players who deserve credit.

At Little Dot Studios, Steph Watts and Harold McShiel have been the perfect producing partners, while Dan Jones, Annie Hughes and Catherine Bray have offered continued support and inspiration, as did our much-missed boss, Andy Taylor.

Artist Sophie Mo and composer Anthony Ing crafted a visual and sonic identity for the podcast, for which we're forever grateful. We're also thankful to past audio wizards Lister Rossel and Jamie Maisner for editing our conversations together.

For joining us on our podcast journey, thank you to Robbie Collin, Beth Webb, Iana Murray, Alex Dudok de Wit and Paul Williams. For their kind support in helping us with this book, thank you to Sam Clements and Jason Wood. And for helping the podcast take flight, thank you to John Harris and the team at Acast.

For helping us navigate the expansive world of Studio Ghibli, we must thank Evan Ma, Yoshiaki Nishimura, Jeff Wexler, Steve Alpert, Michaël Dudok de Wit, Helen McCarthy and Andrew Osmond.

As Western Ghibli fans we must thank those at StudioCanal, GKIDS and Elysian Film Group, without whom we wouldn't have been able to watch any of these wonderful films in the first place. Thank you to Carys Gaskin, Thom Leaman, Dave Jesteadt, Lucy Rubin, Zoe Flower and Nick McKay.

Thank you to Julia Wrigley and David Cox at Film4, who let us make the podcast in the first place, and to Roland Hall and Ross Hamilton at Welbeck Publishing for letting us turn that podcast into a book.

And thank you to Mim, Ivo and Louisa for their incredible and ongoing support for two grown men who only want to talk about cartoons.

Published in 2021 by Welbeck

An Imprint of Welbeck Non-Fiction Limited, part of Welbeck Publishing Group
20 Mortimer Street London W1T 3JW

Text © 2021 Little Dot Studios Limited, written by Michael Leader & Jake Cunningham
Design © 2021 Welbeck Non-fiction Limited

A CIP catalogue record for this book is available from the British Library

ISBN 978 1 78739 665 4

Printed in Dubai

10 9 8 7 6 5 4 3 2

MIX
Paper from responsible sources
FSC® C004800
www.fsc.org

ジブリ文庫

# GHIBLIOTHEQUE

## AN UNOFFICIAL GUIDE TO THE MOVIES
## OF STUDIO GHIBLI

MICHAEL LEADER & JAKE CUNNINGHAM

FROM THE LITTLE DOT STUDIOS PODCAST

WELBECK

# CONTENTS

# INTRODUCTION

IF YOU LOOK UP THE HEAD OFFICE OF JAPANESE ANIMATION LEGENDS STUDIO GHIBLI ON GOOGLE MAPS, THE LEAD IMAGE YOU SEE IS OF AN A4 PRINTOUT SIGN POSTED IN A WINDOW: "THIS IS NOT GHIBLI MUSEUM. IT'S STUDIO GHIBLI OFFICE. NOT OPEN TO PUBLIC." NOT THAT WE CARED, WE KNEW PRECISELY WHERE WE WERE, AND WHY WE WERE THERE.

But who are we, anyway? We're Michael Leader and Jake Cunningham. Back in 2018, we started working in the same office together. Both obsessed with film, podcasts and film podcasts, our eventual collaboration seemed inevitable: all that was needed was the perfect meet-cute moment. Then, a conversation across the desk revealed a heinous, monumental gap in Jake's cultural knowledge: he'd barely seen any Studio Ghibli films. Well, this simply would not do – at least not on Michael's watch.

An avowed Ghibli fanatic, Michael planned out a rigorous and robust syllabus for Jake, a guided tour through the Studio's entire catalogue, along the way taking in their historic successes (*Spirited Away*, *My Neighbour Totoro*, *Princess Mononoke*), fan favourites (*Kiki's Delivery Service*, *Grave of the Fireflies*, *Pom Poko*) and deepest cuts (*Ocean Waves*, *My Neighbours the Yamadas*, *The Red Turtle*).

And why not capture it all on microphone? The resulting podcast would strike a balance between Michael's anorak-level research into the production history, the industry context, and the people and personalities behind the films, and Jake's fresh, unfettered take, experiencing these classics of world cinema as a first-time viewer, one film at a time. All that was needed was an *ever so slightly* laboured but undeniably catchy (and surprisingly tricky to spell) pun title, playing on the French word for library – *bibliothèque* – suggesting a warm, welcoming setting for this regular film club.

**Opposite:** The exterior of the Ghibli Museum in Mitaka, Tokyo.

**Above, Left to Right:** Chihiro looking ahead to her adventure in *Spirited Away*; Jake and Michael in the midst of their adventure at Ghibli Museum; Hayao Miyazaki, hard at work, in the documentary *Never Ending Man: Hayao Miyazaki*.

**Above:** Inside the Ghibli Museum. To the right stands Mr Dough, the rising star of Miyazaki's short film *Mr Dough and the Egg Princess*, which only screens at the museum.

**Opposite:** Fans from around the world make a pilgrimage to the Ghibli Museum for a chance to be transported into the world of Ghibli.

**Overleaf:** One of the attractions at the Ghibli Museum is a walkthrough diorama of an animator's workshop.

Twenty-odd films and six thousand miles later, Jake had been brought up to speed, and both of us, with co-producers Steph Watts and Harold McShiel in tow, travelled out to Tokyo for the ultimate Ghibli pilgrimage. On this trip, we would sink our teeth into immaculately crafted pastries in the shape of Ghibli's world-famous, instantly recognizable mascot, Totoro; we would walk in the footsteps of the young lovers from Ghibli gem (and Michael's favourite film of the bunch) *Whisper of the Heart*; we would meet and talk with Ghibli veterans; and we would scour every inch of Tokyo for a rare poster of director Isao Takahata's adult-skewing animated drama,

*Only Yesterday.* (Which we would eventually find, much to Jake's beaming delight, tucked away in a cramped print stall in the nerd nirvana that is Nakano Broadway.) We would also visit the magical Ghibli Museum, a monument to the beguiling imaginative worlds created by one of the world's greatest animation studios, as well as to the artform of animation itself.

But, as Google would happily tell us, the building we were looking at then was very clearly *not* the Ghibli Museum. This was an office complex on a nondescript street in a quiet area of town, and on this morning in November 2019, the unmistakable company logo out front was even obscured by an overgrown hedge. But we knew, behind those doors is where the magic happens. As we watched employees filing in through the doors, some stopping to ask us in hesitant English if we were lost ("Thank you but, no, honestly, we're not!"), we knew that another Miyazaki masterpiece – the still-forthcoming *How Do You Live?* – was being painstakingly hand-crafted, at the glacial pace of one minute of animation per month. Some people climb Kilimanjaro, walk the Great Wall, visit the Vatican; we came here.

This book is a culmination of over three years of venturing deep into the enchanted and enchanting world of Studio Ghibli, reflecting our comprehensive, two-pronged approach to each film and the overarching story they weave about Ghibli's two founding filmmakers, directors Hayao Miyazaki and Isao Takahata, their stalwart producer Toshio Suzuki, and their singular, influential, world-conquering work.

From 1984's *Nausicaä of the Valley of the Wind* to 2020's *Earwig and the Witch*, *Ghibliotheque* is an all-encompassing overview of Studio Ghibli's feature work. Like the podcast before it, each chapter of this book kicks off with a generous slab of background intel from Michael, before Jake delivers his in-depth, film-fan reaction. We'd like to think that, individually, these chapters give a deep insight in to some of the most beloved animated films ever made, maybe even inspiring you to dig further into the Studio's back catalogue if you haven't, or revisit some old favourites if you have.

As a whole, though, *Ghibliotheque* pieces together the narrative and thematic puzzle that is Studio Ghibli – the larger-than-life personalities behind the films, and how they're reflected both in and between the lines of the work. The first thirty-five years of Studio Ghibli chart the rise and rise of a production company, the maturation of two very enigmatic

HAYAO MIYAZAKI WROTE IN HIS PROPOSAL THAT THE GHIBLI MUSEUM WOULD BE: "A MUSEUM THAT IS INTERESTING AND WHICH RELAXES THE SOUL. A MUSEUM WHERE MUCH CAN BE DISCOVERED. A MUSEUM BASED ON A CLEAR AND CONSISTENT PHILOSOPHY. A MUSEUM WHERE THOSE SEEKING ENJOYMENT CAN ENJOY, THOSE SEEKING TO PONDER CAN PONDER, AND THOSE SEEKING TO FEEL CAN FEEL. A MUSEUM THAT MAKES YOU FEEL MORE ENRICHED WHEN YOU LEAVE THAN WHEN YOU ENTERED!"

祝　起工　ジブリパーク

geniuses, the friction between them and their younger colleagues, and the rousing of an animation giant both in Japan and, very slowly, abroad.

When Michael first fell in love with Ghibli, few of their films were available in the UK, and there was very little authoritative, serious writing for a blossoming fanatic to read. With that in mind, we must nod to the Ghibli critics, historians and fellow travellers who have helped shape our view of the Studio and their work, with thanks to Helen McCarthy, Jonathan Clements, Susan Napier, Andrew Osmond, Roger Ebert, Jonathan Ross, Robbie Collin, Nick Bradshaw, David Jenkins, Alex Dudok de Wit and Rayna Denison.

Now, thanks to the efforts of companies such as StudioCanal and GKIDS, and the landmark acquisition of the Ghibli library by Netflix and HBO Max, almost every feature is available, at the touch of a button, on disc or digital. Studio Ghibli's films, at least internationally, are more accessible than ever, but there is still so much to learn. Look for Studio Ghibli in a bookshop in the UK or US and, if you're lucky, you'll find half a shelf. In Japan you'd find a whole floor-to-ceiling bookcase. So, while, at time of writing this is the first book on Ghibli in English to have such a broad scope, we can only scratch the surface.

There is still so much ground to cover that we haven't touched on here – Ghibli-related short films, commercials, spin-offs, unrealized projects and collaborations, even a video game, *Ni No Kuni*. There's the Ghibli Museum, and the upcoming Ghibli theme park, not to mention so many key figures, insights, anecdotes and mountains of merchandise that will have to wait for another day. And what about the careers of Ghibli filmmakers either side of their time with Ghibli – from the groundbreaking early anime of Isao Takahata and Hayao

Miyazaki, to the continuing work of Hiromasa Yonebayashi and Studio Ponoc?

For the sake of space, time and our very wellbeing, we remained focused on the core feature films made by Studio Ghibli, sticking true to the spirit that has guided the podcast from the beginning: here's our take on what's readily available, legally, right now. If you'd like to go deeper, come back and we'll go further.

For now, whether you're a Jake or a Michael; whether you know your Ponyo from your Porco Rosso; whether you've seen all, or one, or none of these films, let *Ghibliotheque* be your guide.

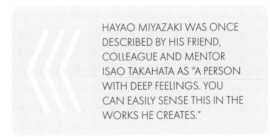

HAYAO MIYAZAKI WAS ONCE DESCRIBED BY HIS FRIEND, COLLEAGUE AND MENTOR ISAO TAKAHATA AS "A PERSON WITH DEEP FEELINGS. YOU CAN EASILY SENSE THIS IN THE WORKS HE CREATES."

**Above:** Hayao Miyazaki's son, Goro Miyazaki (left), at the ground-breaking ceremony for the Ghibli theme park in Nagakute in Aichi Prefecture. Now a veteran director, Goro started as a landscaper and first joined Ghibli to found and run the Ghibli Museum.

**Opposite:** The Never Ending Man himself, Hayao Miyazaki.

# NAUSICAÄ OF THE VALLEY OF THE WIND (KAZE NO TANI NO NAUSHIKA, 1984)

## THE FIRST WIND RISES

DIRECTED BY: HAYAO MIYAZAKI
WRITTEN BY: HAYAO MIYAZAKI
LENGTH: 1HR 57MIN
RELEASE DATE (JAPAN): 11 MARCH 1984

PICKING A BEGINNING FOR THE STORY OF STUDIO GHIBLI IS A TRICKY TASK, BUT WHERE THEIR FEATURE FILM OUTPUT IS CONCERNED, THERE IS ONE CRUCIAL STARTING POINT. 1984'S *NAUSICAÄ OF THE VALLEY OF THE WIND* ISN'T A STUDIO GHIBLI FILM IN NAME, BUT ITS CONCEPTION, PRODUCTION AND EVENTUAL SUCCESS WOULD LEAD DIRECTLY TO THE FOUNDING OF THE STUDIO THE FOLLOWING YEAR, AND LATER ON IT WOULD BE RETROACTIVELY ADDED TO THE STUDIO GHIBLI CANON, BOTH IN JAPAN AND INTERNATIONALLY.

But let's start in 1979. By this point, Hayao Miyazaki was already a veteran of the Japanese animation industry with a history of credits stretching back to the early 1960s, including work on popular series such as *Future Boy Conan*, *3000 Leagues in Search of Mother* and *Heidi: Girl of the Alps*. Miyazaki also had a hand in the anime adaptation of Monkey Punch's perennially popular master thief manga *Lupin III*, and had scored his first credit as a feature director with the Lupin spin-off, *Lupin III: The Castle of Cagliostro*. The film was received well by critics, and became quite an influential film among young animators, but it didn't make much of a dent at the Japanese box office.

One place where *The Castle of Cagliostro* did have an impact, though, was at *Animage* magazine. Since its launch in May 1978, *Animage* had been championing Japanese animation and manga, and Toshio Suzuki, one of the magazine's editors, was a strong supporter of Miyazaki and his work.

**Opposite:** Nausicaä flies through the Valley of the Wind, and onto screens, in Ghibli's first feature.
**Above:** The environmental themes that would become a defining feature of Miyazaki's work with Ghibli have their roots in *Nausicaä of the Valley of the Wind*'s post-apocalyptic landscape.

In the early 1980s, Yasuyoshi Tokuma, the president of Tokuma Shoten, the publishers of *Animage*, discussed a plan to create projects that mixed film, music and print media. Suzuki saw his chance and now admits he got "a little greedy and ambitious", bringing Miyazaki into Tokuma Shoten with the idea for them to back his second feature film. However, as Suzuki recalls:

"They said you could never have a hit with a film that wasn't based on an original work. When I told Miyazaki about it, he had a good answer. 'Well, let's make an original work, then.'"

The eureka moment came when Suzuki and Miyazaki decided to publish a manga in the pages of *Animage*, with the hope of then adapting it into a feature film. In February 1982,

*Nausicaä of the Valley of the Wind* launched, and it quickly became one of the magazine's most popular features. The top brass at Tokuma Shoten finally took notice, and encouraged Miyazaki to develop the manga series into a feature film.

Toshio Suzuki would serve as part of the production committee for the *Nausicaä* film, but Hayao Miyazaki had only one person in mind to be the film's producer: his mentor Isao Takahata. Miyazaki and Takahata's relationship was formed at Toei Animation in the 1960s, after they met at a union committee meeting. A radical at heart, Takahata approached the production of his first feature film, known as *Little Norse Prince* in the UK (*Horus, Prince of the Sun* in the US), as a collective endeavour, allowing junior staff members to chip in with story ideas and character designs or, in young Hayao Miyazaki's case, get their first taste of designing scenes as well as animating them. The experience was foundational for Miyazaki:

"I actually learned how to do that work during the process of making the film... it wasn't a case of

木々を愛で
虫と語り
風をまねく鳥の人……

原作・脚本・監督／宮崎駿
風の谷のナウシカ
製作／株徳間書店・博報堂書配給／東映株　NAUSICAA

THE ENORMOUS INSECTOID OHMU (ABOVE) ARE THE FIRST IN GHIBLI'S LONG SEEMINGLY-ROGUES' GALLERY OF FANTASTICAL, FEROCIOUS AND BEAUTIFULLY DESIGNED CREATURES, WHILE NAUSICAÄ IS THE STUDIO'S FIRST LANDMARK FEMALE PROTAGONIST. THE STORY OF BOTH THE OHMU AND NAUSICAÄ IS CONTINUED IN THE *NAUSICAÄ OF THE VALLEY OF THE WIND* MANGA SERIES, CONTINUED BY MIYAZAKI UNTIL 1994.

implementing what I already knew; I was feeling my way as I worked on the project."

The creative partnership would continue, inspiring generations with series ranging from *Lupin III* to *Future Boy Conan*. Miyazaki saw the value in bringing his old partner on board to help bring *Nausicaä* to the big screen. The only trouble was, Takahata wasn't interested.

Toshio Suzuki recalls being taken out on a very out of character sake bender by Miyazaki after he heard the news: "This was a side of Miyazaki I had never seen before. Naturally, he got drunk, and before I knew it, he was crying. The tears didn't stop... He said, 'I devoted my youth to Takahata, but he has never done anything for me.'"

Suzuki claims he finally talked Takahata around to producing *Nausicaä*, thereby bringing together three of the cornerstones of what would eventually become Studio Ghibli. One of Takahata's major contributions to the project would provide the other, when he helped pick experimental composer Joe Hisaishi to compose the film's soundtrack. Hisaishi has scored every Miyazaki film since.

In 1983, Hayao Miyazaki wrote his directorial statement for the *Nausicaä* film, highlighting themes that will resound throughout Ghibli's work:

"For the past few years, I have put forth ideas for film projects with the following ethos: to offer a sense of liberation to present-day young people who, in this suffocating, overprotective, and managed society, find their path to self-reliant independence blocked and have become neurotic... Can hope exist even during this twilight era?"

However, even with all the constituent parts in place, production was far from smooth. Isao Takahata's soon-to-be legendary status as having "descended from a giant sloth" was in full effect, and the project had trouble meeting deadlines.

At one point, a job listing was posted in *Animage* asking for extra hands to join the crew to speed up the animation process, and one respondent was a young Hideaki Anno, who, as the story goes, reportedly turned up at the studio, knocked on Miyazaki's office door, and handed him some sample storyboards that impressed the director to such an extent that the newcomer was assigned the responsibility of animating perhaps the most important (and, in the end, visually impactful) sequence of the film, featuring the unstable, decaying "God Warrior". Anno would work again with Ghibli, and would be seen as one of Miyazaki's many protégés, before becoming an anime legend in his own right as creator of the blockbuster series *Neon Genesis Evangelion*.

Released in Japan in March 1984, *Nausicaä of the Valley of the Wind* was an instant hit, selling close to a million tickets, making a strong case for spectacular, feature-length Japanese animation, and proving Suzuki right: there was a future in the fantasies of Hayao Miyazaki.

## WARRIORS OF THE WIND?

*Nausicaä* was also, controversially, the first Miyazaki film to be released in the US. Roger Corman's New World Pictures acquired the film, recut it and remodelled it as more of a family-friendly fantasy adventure in the *Star Wars* mould, unleashing it in cinemas in 1985 under the new title *Warriors of the Wind*. The experience would influence Ghibli's relationship with international releases for years to come.

She is a friend of the Earth.
1000 years from now...a time when evil overruns the world and our only hope for the future is in the hands of a Princess and those who follow her.

WARRIORS OF THE WIND

It might not have the studio logo at the start, but there's no denying who made this film. From its headstrong, youthful female protagonist, to its lush green fields, to its moral exploration of militarism and message of environmental harmony, *Nausicaä of the Valley of the Wind* is clearly a Ghibli film, made before Ghibli even existed. It's a foundational text, that is very much a foundation. Rich in ambition both creatively and narratively, the film is beautifully constructed, sprawling in scope and in message, but it never quite coalesces in story and style like some of the studio's later films. As a first chapter though, it's an exceptional start.

*Nausicaä* is a hazier film than a lot of Ghibli's work; in this post-apocalyptic landscape, sea, sky and land overlap in blue hues, as if the natural world here has been tortured so much that its own boundaries have crumbled. The outlines of the characters are slightly trimmer than in other Ghibli productions as well, softly resting against their backgrounds rather than popping out from them, as if they too are being sucked into the decaying environment. After being established for years by Hayao Miyazaki in *Animage* magazine, the world of *Nausicaä* is fully realized, the scale of fictional history enormous, but never unwieldy. It is as if the ancient tapestry of the world has been unfurled, and while we might be able to sharply see what's been rolled out directly in front of us, we can still see either end, imagining the threads that show how we got here, and where we might go.

This world, featuring giant skulls that punctuate landscapes, poisonous snowfall, huge, mutated insects and toxic seas may initially appear alien, but it's an alien world that feels identifiable. The Sea of Decay, which has supposedly succumbed to the toxicity, has a forest of trunks beneath it, webbed together like a nervous system, the planet itself being almost anthropomorphic. The titular Valley of the Wind feels like a rural European patchwork (much like the towns Ghibli would create in *Kiki's Delivery Service* and *Howl's Moving Castle*), made up of Dutch windmills and Nordic style, tucked within the French alps. Contrast is provided by the soldiers who invade the peaceful valley, who wear medieval armour and whose planes feel lifted from a World War II engineer's sketchbook (Miyazaki's admiration for a skilled pilot in a slick red plane debuted here, not in *Porco Rosso*, you know). This careful balance of fantasy and normality means *Nausicaä* benefits from the empathy that audiences manufacture as they spot the recognizable, and the excitement that comes from the imaginary.

Nausicaä herself is pragmatic, patient, compassionate and has an intense affinity with nature, placing her at the start of a great lineage of Ghibli protagonists, from Kiki to Chihiro and many others. In one of the film's many quiet, meditative moments, she uses the thick, transparent cornea of a giant insect called an Ohm, to simultaneously protect herself from, and observe, the snow-like fall of toxic spores. Despite the danger the natural world could inflict, she appreciates its beauty;

similarly, when a fox squirrel – which looks like an electric Pokémon with the markings of the catbus from *My Neighbour Totoro* – bites her, she understands that it is simply scared and offers it safety, ultimately taming the creature. In this world, most people view the natural world and its potential to damage as an attack on humanity, but Nausicaä understands that the natural world is *defending* itself against humanity.

In addition to her compassion, Nausicaä has a fearless fighting spirit, single-handedly taking on batches of murderous royal guards at a time. She also guides troops through a spectacular, bullet-frenzied, explosion-battered air battle, which is one of Ghibli's finest action sequences (featuring a plane, launching from inside another plane, while on fire – it's something that sounds more *Fast and Furious* than Studio Ghibli). On the ground, Hideaki Anno's animation of the God Warrior – a biomechanical weapon of mass destruction, who previously destroyed much of the planet, and whose existence creates more division than unification – is a slippery, unsettling and grotesque work, a gloopy Godzilla that is both terrifying and pathetic.

**Above:** Masks are not optional when flying in the Sea of Waste.

**Opposite:** Nausicaä's companion, a fox-squirrel hybrid called Teto, points towards Miyazaki's flair for furry familiars, which would sustain Ghibli's merchandise empire in the years to come.

A perfect companion alongside the more meditative moments and the bombastic ones, is the first score from Ghibli's legendary composer Joe Hisaishi. Hisaishi wrestles his efforts between experimental, pulsing synth jazz and soaring orchestration, with a whisper of George Frideric Handel. The result is a surprising, epic fusion that feels as much like *The Lord of the Rings* as it does Donna Summer's disco behemoth version of 'MacArthur Park'. It is ambitious, hitting high points that are on par with the best in the library, but its bolder synth moments can be more jarring than complementary, and while admirable, it is occasionally unfocused.

The same could be said for the film as a whole. The antagonist Kushana lacks complexity and can easily be pigeonholed as "the villain" – a role that would become harder to define in later Ghibli films – her prosthetic arm a disappointing and obvious signpost for viewers. Additionally, in its final moments, a messianic resolve attempts to tie a pleasantly misshapen moral package together with a bow that doesn't quite fit. A bolder, more open and more satisfying ending would come in *Princess Mononoke*, when a homogenized exploration of the relationship between warfare, environmentalism, humanity and fantasy would perfect what *Nausicaä* began. Still though, what an opening chapter.

# LAPUTA: CASTLE IN THE SKY (TENKŪ NO SHIRO RAPYUTA, 1986)

## STUDIO GHIBLI TAKES FLIGHT

DIRECTED BY: HAYAO MIYAZAKI
WRITTEN BY: HAYAO MIYAZAKI
LENGTH: 2HR 5MIN
RELEASE DATE (JAPAN): 2 AUGUST 1986

ON JUNE 15, 1985, STUDIO GHIBLI WAS BORN. HOWEVER, THE COMPANY WAS FORMED JUST AS MUCH OUT OF NECESSITY AS AMBITION. FOLLOWING THE BLOCKBUSTER SUCCESS OF *NAUSICAÄ OF THE VALLEY OF THE WIND*, HAYAO MIYAZAKI AND ISAO TAKAHATA HAD TROUBLE SECURING FINANCING AND FINDING A PRODUCTION PARTNER TO CREATE YET MORE HIGHLY POLISHED, FEATURE-LENGTH ANIMATED FILMS. AND SO, THEY STRUCK OUT ON THEIR OWN.

The name came from Miyazaki, a lifelong aeroplane enthusiast, nodding to an Italian reconnaissance aircraft in World War II which, in turn, was named after the warm Saharan winds that sweep across the Mediterranean. Studio Ghibli, too, would be a fresh, creative force blowing through the Japanese animation industry.

Tokuma Shoten, publishers of *Animage* and backers of *Nausicaä of the Valley of the Wind*, gave the fledgling company start-up support, while *Animage* editor Toshio Suzuki would moonlight in an unofficial capacity at the newly founded Ghibli – even printing his own business cards.

Rather than the safe bet of a sequel to *Nausicaä*, Studio Ghibli's first feature project would be a return to the younger-skewing fantasy adventure genre that Miyazaki excelled at with the 1978 series *Future Boy Conan*. Drawing influence from *Gulliver's Travels* and the writing of Jules Verne, Miyazaki's original December 1984 proposal for what would eventually become *Laputa: Castle in the Sky* included provisional titles that hinted at this direction: "Young Pazu and the Mystery of the Levitation Crystal", "Flying Treasure Island"

and "The Flying Empire". The film, Miyazaki writes, would be an "intensely thrilling classic action film" that would "bring animation back to its roots".

As the film would be a retro-futuristic throwback to nineteenth-century science fiction with a steampunk style aesthetic, producer Isao Takahata suggested that Miyazaki make a research trip to the UK, to visit one of the birthplaces of the Industrial Revolution. There, Miyazaki took a trip to Wales to see both the rolling landscape of the valleys and its coal mining industry first-hand, but it was the sense of community that would influence him the most. His visit coincided with the conflict between miners' unions and Margaret Thatcher's Conservative government, when long-term strike action had been defeated by Westminster, resulting in widespread unemployment and poverty across the region. Miyazaki would

**Opposite:** *Castle in the Sky's* young protagonists, Sheeta and Pazu, soar above the flying island of Laputa.

**Below:** Sheeta and Pazu lie down in the grass, a restful setting for many Ghibli moments.

later recall, in a 1999 interview with Helen McCarthy for *Manga Max* magazine:

"I really admired the way the miners' unions fought to the very end for their jobs and communities, and I wanted to reflect the strength of those communities in my film. I saw so many places with abandoned machinery, abandoned mines – the fabric of the industry was there, but no people. It made a strong impression on me. A whole industry with no people."

Released in August 1986, *Castle in the Sky* didn't fare as well at the box office as *Nausicaä of the Valley of the Wind*, selling only two-thirds as many tickets as its predecessor on initial theatrical release. However, its reputation would grow with time, and its cultural impact would be felt across animation and video games, not least in the long-running Japanese role-playing video game series *Final Fantasy*. *Castle in the Sky*'s soundtrack albums, composed by Ghibli stalwart Joe Hisaishi, became bestsellers, and the film amassed a cult following over the years thanks to home video releases and regular screenings on television.

*Castle in the Sky*'s life on the small screen gives Ghibli its most curious tradition and landmark. When the film screens on Japanese television, it has become customary for viewers to take to Twitter and post the word "balse" when that magic phrase is uttered towards the end of the film. Such is the popularity of the film that, in August 2013, fans managed to break the record for the most tweets posted in a single second. During that screening, there was a spike of over 140,000 tweets when the fateful line was spoken, compared to the usual average, at the time, of 5,700 posts a second.

Studio Ghibli's first film might not have been an instant success, but the winds of change blowing through the industry were gaining strength.

**Above:** The fabled island of Laputa.

**Opposite:** The Japanese-language poster for *Laputa: Castle in the Sky*.

## GHIBLI OR JIBLI?

The eternal question. The endless debate. The topic that's sure to turn any Ghibli conversation sour. How do you pronounce "Ghibli" – an Italian word, borrowed by the Japanese, and then translated into English – anyway? Is it "Gibli"... or "Jibli"? In his memoir *Mixing Work with Pleasure*, Toshio Suzuki closes the book on the topic quite definitively: "Incidentally, the Japanese pronunciation of the word 'Ghibli', which is Italian in origin, was phonetically wrong; it should have been '*giburi*' instead of '*jiburi*'. It is a little too late to correct it now, though."

**Left:** Miyazaki's design for the giant Laputan robot has its roots in his work on the anime series *Lupin III*, and was reportedly inspired by a Fleischer Studios Superman short from 1941 titled *The Mechanical Monsters*.

**Above:** Pazu and Sheeta desperately hold on to the airborne island.

At the Studio Ghibli museum, if you visit the Saturn Cinema, you might be lucky enough to see *Imaginary Flying Machines*, the 2002 short film written, directed and voiced by Hayao Miyazaki, originally made as a companion to an exhibition about *Laputa: Castle in the Sky*. It's a whirlwind review of mechanical flight in myriad forms, with animation's biggest aerophile Miyazaki (styled like Porco Rosso) as our guide through airborne creations from his own mind and those of other artists. The short feels like a soaring slideshow update of the opening titles to *Castle in the Sky*, which years earlier, in a line etching style as if lifted from ancient texts, showcased Miyazaki's enduring love of flying vehicles. In revisiting the style of its title sequence years later, Miyazaki reminds us again not just of his passion for planes, but for *Castle in the Sky*. It was the first film to be made by the officially formed Studio Ghibli and is an exhibition of what Ghibli would become.

Following downwind from *Nausicaä*, *Castle in the Sky* is tonally lighter than its more world-weary forebear; the humble heroes Pazu and Sheeta are youthful and sparky, with the purity of heart that comes with a true kids' adventure story. Pazu is a young miner, thrilled as much by the inner workings of a mineshaft as he is by his flock of birds and trumpet playing. Sheeta is a forthright farm girl who is secretly a princess and begins the film tumbling through the sky, before – with the help of her glowing necklace that allows her to levitate – being rescued by Pazu. With this magical sky-diving meet-cute out

of the way, together they race to the mystical floating city of Laputa, while being chased by the villainous Colonel Muska and the not-so-villainous pirate Dola.

Pratfalls, wisecracks and a sequence involving escalating feats of muscular prowess are cartoonish, hilarious and show the Miyazaki who cut his teeth with the comically elastic characters of hugely popular anime film and TV series *Lupin III*. The design of the city of Laputa also recalls this work, in particular the Romanesque columns and waterways from the spectacular finale of Miyazaki's feature film debut *Lupin III: The Castle of Cagliostro*, which find themselves transported to the grounds of this castle in the sky. Although an appearance of a fox squirrel from *Nausicaä* may further suggest that the film might only be cribbing from the past, *Castle in the Sky* brings new ideas of style, characterisation and thematic development that would stick with the studio.

Kiki wouldn't make her debut for a while and when she did, she had clearly been using the Sheeta style guide, her distinct red hairband and loose dark dress on show here, three years before *Kiki's Delivery Service* was released. Motro, a pirate engineer with a brush of a moustache and circular spectacles gruffly cranks away at machinery, very similarly to how Kamajī the boiler man in *Spirited Away* would in years to come. As for the camphor tree that blooms over the top of Totoro's magical forest, that was two years away, but look at the great tree at the centre of Laputa and you'll see its ancestral roots. Additionally,

a simple fried egg, cooked to perfection, placed on thick hunks of bread and peacefully shared between friends is an early course of Ghibli food at its best. It's been carefully prepared, but not lavishly made and, as with many of Ghibli's finest food moments that would follow, it is served in commune; the taste, the trust and the moment of calm all equally felt.

It might be more playful than *Nausicaä*, but thematically *Castle in the Sky* continues to explore ideas of environmentalism and warfare that Miyazaki would carry throughout his career. In a magnificent moment, one of the caves beneath Pazu's mining town is shown to glow with as much spectacle and sublimity as the night sky; Miyazaki revering the earth beneath our feet with the same wonder that might be held for the stars above us. On Laputa itself, while the landscape becomes a battleground and the industrial parts of the city break apart, it is the natural roots – considered by the villain Muska to be a virus – that save our heroes.

In a rare character misstep Colonel Muska is a brazen

militarist and disappointingly one-note for a Ghibli antagonist. However the Robots, a heartbreaking metallic creation of destructive power and innocent protectiveness (not dissimilar to the central figure in *The Iron Giant*), are a more curious creation. They can be controlled to become a weapon, but in their moments of independence they are shown to be peaceful caretakers of nature. Despite the violence we see them inflict, the Robots still feel like a symbol of peace, a dichotomy that Miyazaki would continue to explore for years, most directly in wartime drama *The Wind Rises*. A further military message comes in the form of Pazu and Sheeta's aircraft, a nimble glider that floats high above the army and pirates and is first to land at Laputa, showing that the plane that has no weapons can be the one that's ultimately rewarded. It may grapple with murky topics, but the thrills always remain the focus, particularly helped by Joe Hisaishi's exceptional balancing of synth and orchestration to perfectly hit his three-word brief of "dreams, romance, adventure".

Miyazaki said that he wanted to recreate his "childhood dreams" with the film, and in soaring moments it does feel like they're no longer just imaginary flying machines, they're Miyazaki's dreams come to life.

**Above:** Studio Ghibli magic, as worn by Sheeta.

**Opposite:** The young heroes Sheeta and Pazu find themselves caught in the centre of adventure – and the firing line.

# MY NEIGHBOUR TOTORO (TONARI NO TOTORO, 1988)

## THE BIRTH OF AN ICON

DIRECTED BY: HAYAO MIYAZAKI
WRITTEN BY: HAYAO MIYAZAKI
LENGTH: 2HR 5MIN
RELEASE DATE (JAPAN): 2 AUGUST 1986

IF YOU SUBSCRIBE TO THE SOMEWHAT REDUCTIVE NOTION THAT HAYAO MIYAZAKI IS JAPAN'S ANSWER TO WALT DISNEY OR STEVEN SPIELBERG, THE FURRY FOREST TROLL TOTORO IS UNDENIABLY HIS MICKEY MOUSE, HIS E.T. THE EXTRA-TERRESTRIAL. TOTORO IS AN ICON FOR GENERATIONS OF JAPANESE CHILDREN AND – CRUCIALLY – AN EASILY MERCHANDISABLE MONEY-SPINNER, WHOSE ROTUND, WELCOMING FORM CAN BE EFFORTLESSLY REMOULDED INTO CUDDLY TOYS, COSY NIGHTLIGHTS AND OVERSIZED, EXCEEDINGLY COMFORTABLE SLIPPERS.

Totoro graces Studio Ghibli's own logo, and would become their brand ambassador abroad, popping up in cameo form in Western media ranging from *Toy Story 3* and *The Simpsons* to the comic book pages of *X-Men* and *The Sandman*. However, in the late 1980s, Totoro was merely an acorn from which the Studio Ghibli empire would grow.

After two epic anime features that traded on fantasy settings and spectacular scenes of often violent derring-do, Hayao Miyazaki envisaged his next project as something more low-key and child-friendly. "*My Neighbour Totoro* aims to be a happy and heart-warming film," wrote Miyazaki in his

directorial statement, "a film that lets the audience go home with pleasant, good feelings."

Crucially, after two films based in fictional worlds created from a patchwork of mostly Western storytelling influences, *My Neighbour Totoro* would see Miyazaki turning his attention to a uniquely Japanese setting and story. He lamented that

**Above:** Mei meets her new neighbour.
**Opposite:** A tale of two families: sisters Mei and Satsuki spend time with the Totoro clan.

"Though we live in Japan, and are without doubt Japanese, we continue to create animation films that avoid depicting Japan." Therefore, with this post-war tale of a friendship between two young girls and the forest spirits living near to their new home in the countryside, Miyazaki would hope to capture "what we have forgotten, what we don't notice, what we are convinced we have lost".

Initially, Studio Ghibli's financiers at their parent company, Tokuma Shoten, weren't interested in a twee adventure with a friendly forest troll – they wanted another fantasy adventure with an exotic-sounding foreign-language title in the vein of *Laputa: Castle in the Sky* or *Nausicaä of the Valley of the Wind*.

And so, it initially looked like *My Neighbour Totoro* might end up as a shorter, straight-to-video feature. But when Toshio Suzuki secured funding for *Grave of the Fireflies*, the

first Ghibli feature from Studio co-founder Isao Takahata, from Shinchosha, the publishers of the source novel, the mastermind producer saw an opportunity to use patriarchal, hierarchy-obsessed Japanese business practices to the studio's advantage. Suzuki's scheme was as follows:

"The plan was for Shinchosha and Tokuma to join hands and each create a movie that they would release as a double feature. Shinchosha has a longer history than Tokuma, and since that's the kind of thing that presidents of publishing companies really care about, President Tokuma would have to accept if the president of Shinchosha requested it."

A deal was struck, and the fledgling Studio found themselves with two films in production: *Grave of the Fireflies* from Takahata, and the now feature-length *My Neighbour Totoro* from Miyazaki, poised for a double-bill theatrical release in April 1988. "And the rest," Suzuki noted, "was quite easy."

Well, until the films were actually released, that is...

While the audacious double-bill gambit succeeded in getting both features financed, the films themselves were more critical hits than blockbusters. Together, they took home a special prize at the Blue Ribbon Awards, and *Totoro* itself was awarded Best Film by the prestigious Japanese film magazine *Kinema Junpo*.

However, *My Neighbour Totoro*'s decent, if not spectacular,

**Opposite, Above:** Miyazaki magic so often rises out of the everyday landscape around us.

**Opposite, Below:** Totoro delights in the simple pleasure of raindrops landing on an umbrella.

**Below:** Joe Hisaishi's themes from *Totoro* have become standards in their own right, performed in concerts around the world to sell-out audiences. Here, the score is performed in Paris in 2011.

initial performance at the box office would soon be dwarfed by its takings from home video releases and, crucially, merchandizing. It wasn't until 1990 that the Studio saw the value in licensing the character, but ultimately billions would be made from Totoro toys and other assorted tie-ins, as the character's reputation snowballed from cute creation to national icon.

Internationally, Totoro took his time to emerge. A screening at the Barbican Centre in London in 1991 predated the film's limited theatrical release in the US in 1993, which came via 50th Street Films, the independent and world cinema-focused distribution subsidiary of the notoriously low-rent "splatstick" horror studio Troma Entertainment. Fox Video released *My Neighbour Totoro* on VHS the following year, sporting subtly Americanized cover artwork and an English dub produced by Streamline Entertainment.

Reports claim that this Fox Video release surpassed 500,000 sales, but, like many early Ghibli films, it wouldn't be until the success of *Spirited Away*, and DVD releases in 2006 from Walt Disney Home Entertainment (in the US) and Optimum Releasing (later StudioCanal, in the UK), that the film's popularity in the English-speaking world really took flight.

A consistent champion over those years was Roger Ebert, the influential American film writer who managed to straddle both broadsheet and broadcast criticism in his work for the *Chicago Sun-Times* and on US TV's *Siskel & Ebert & the Movies*. *My Neighbour Totoro* was just one of the Ghibli films to make his personal "Great Movies" canon, but it's the one that provoked the purest response: "Whenever I watch it, I smile, and smile, and smile."

But perhaps the most unlikely fan was legendary filmmaker Akira Kurosawa, whose peerless body of work, from *Rashomon* to *Seven Samurai*, *Yojimbo* to *Ran*, epitomized Japanese cinema on the world stage. *My Neighbour Totoro* was reportedly on Kurosawa's list of his hundred favourite films, and in a "fireside chat" interview special for television recorded in 1993, the octogenarian left Miyazaki speechless when he interjected:

"You know, I really liked that bus in *Totoro*... Those are the kinds of things that people like me in this business can't do, and that's something I'm really envious about."

Kurosawa also, it's reported, suggested that Miyazaki would have made a great "live-action" filmmaker. To Miyazaki's credit, and our benefit, he wasn't swayed from his path. In fact, he took this remark as something of a backhanded compliment, as if animation were inferior, or simply a stepping stone to live-action filmmaking. Before long, though, Miyazaki's name and work would be as world-renowned as Kurosawa's.

**Above:** Merch-loved. Totoro has been transformed into countless spin-off products, from slippers to sumptuous cream puff treats (as seen here, with Ghibliotheque producers Steph and Harold in the blurry background).

**Previous pages:** Many a Ghibli fan has shouted from the treetops about their love of *My Neighbour Totoro*.

Who is this mysterious girl standing next to Totoro at the bus stop? It's actually the original, sole protagonist of the film as first imagined by Miyazaki. During production he split the character into the two sisters, Mei and Satsuki, but this character lives on in *My Neighbour Totoro*'s iconic poster graphic – now looking like an optical illusion amalgamation of the two beloved characters.

# となりのトトロ

原作・脚本・監督■宮崎 駿

製作■徳間康快 徳間書店作品

このへんないきものは、まだ日本にいるのです。たぶん。

前沢行
稲荷前

*My Neighbour Totoro* is Studio Ghibli. And that's not just because Totoro has been in their studio logo since 1991. It's not just because King Totoro became a mascot for the studio, exporting the brand of Ghibli on an international scale – and a crossover appearance in *Toy Story 3*. It's because it's the quintessence of the studio.

The name "Ghibli" evokes a lot of thoughts: incomparable craftsmanship, soaring musical moments – lots and lots of cats – and comfort. In other works they might animate the occasional disembowelment, treatise on modern warfare or incestuous flirt, yet despite that, Studio Ghibli remains *hygge* for the eyes and ears. If a film studio could be a steaming bowl of ramen on a winter night, that's Ghibli. *My Neighbour Totoro* is that feeling, distilled into eighty-eight perfect minutes. It is a fundamentally joyous experience and, as every viewing seems to unfurl a new wonerful detail, it is one that never tires. It may grapple with haunted houses, death, industrialization and spirituality, but never once do those words feel as heavy as they do on the page, in fact they just drift in the soothing breeze that surrounds a simple story.

In post-war Japan, the Kusakabe family have moved to the countryside. Tatsuo and his two daughters Mei and Satsuki begin living in a rickety old house, while their mother Yasuko is convalescing in a nearby hospital. Next to the house is a forest, with a giant camphor tree at its centre, within which lives a family of forest spirits, who start to interact with Mei and Satsuki. Their adventures range from the seemingly banal, like waiting for a bus, to the sublime, like growing an entire forest in a matter of minutes, but each one is utterly magical.

There is no fear in the world of *My Neighbour Totoro*, or at least when there might be a hint of it, it is quickly scoffed at. When the two girls first arrive at their new home and are told that it's haunted, it's as if they've just got another game to play, more friends to make. They hare around the house, chaotically drifting around corners and hurtling around the garden, and when they discover the "soot-sprites" – halfway between cotton balls and spiders – they joyously scream them away. Now the house can be cleaned, and although there might be a forest spirit nearby, there is the magic of the home to be explored first.

No one does cleaning like Ghibli. In fact, watching someone clean something in a Ghibli film might make you *want* to clean something. Miyazaki allows us to observe the processes of the Kusakabes new life. The hefty lurch of the old-fashioned water pump, the satisfying slide of rags along floorboards and the squelch of clothes being washed under foot. The house itself clangs and clatters in the wind, frightening the girls, so from the comfort of a nice warm bathtub, Tatsuo teaches his daughters to laugh at it, joining the symphony of their new home. We are able to feel the rhythms of domesticity, only later do we notice what has been missing, the girls' mother.

In the hospital, Mei and Satsuki interact with their mother with childlike enthusiasm, but the uncertainties around her illness and timeframe for returning, contrasted with the tone of the girls, underscores the film with a sense of mortality. Whether faced with ghosts, the scary wind sounds that rattle through the house, or their mother's long-term illness, Mei and Satsuki's fearless optimism and sense of adventure is inspiring, regardless of the age of the viewer.

**Left:** A tonsil-eyed view of Mei's first meeting with Totoro.

**Opposite:** Cuddly or creepy? The Catbus might be Miyazaki's most beguiling and bewildering creation of all.

Enter the King. Like all great supporting characters they arrive late, have much less screen time than you remember, but still take over the entire film. When Mei is pottering around the house and garden, she spots a small, white, ghostly shape, like a walking cushion, with pointy ears and big eyes. It meets another similar creature, slightly bigger, this one is blue and is carrying a small, brown bag – naturally Mei is totally unafraid and follows them as they walk into the woods. She finds herself at the foot of the giant camphor tree, and tumbles down a hole, but gets a soft landing – because she's just landed on top of one of the greatest characters in film history.

This is King Totoro. Part cat, part rabbit, part dog, part bear, part owl. That sounds like a creation of Doctor Moreau, it's really not, it's the physical manifestation of that feeling of Ghibli as a whole: instantly comforting. Mei scoots up the furry, barrel chest she's landed on, and stares into King Totoro's eyes; he stares back. Immediate kinship. She scratches him, tickles his nose, he lets out an enormous yawn and they both fall asleep in total peace. This is followed by a shot of a snail climbing a branch, then a water droplet falling into a pond; together they are a capsule of the idealized harmony between fantasy, nature and human that can be seen throughout Miyazaki's work.

In another standout moment in the entire Ghibli oeuvre, the two sisters are found waiting at a bus stop to greet their father. As they wait in the rain, under the rim of her umbrella,

Satsuki spies a large, furry foot, there staring wide-eyed (and sporting a giant leaf as a hat) is King Totoro. She gives him her spare umbrella, and together they wait. The single shot of them awkwardly paused, daring not to look directly at each other, makes the scene iconic; what follows makes it legendary. The lights of King Totoro's bus appear in the distance, but it's not a bus... it's a cat. Well actually, it's both. An inspired surreal creation, with rats for headlights and a 1950s sci-fi sound effect when it slides open its door, the catbus is bewildering. It's glaring grin and cavity of a body might initially seem creepy, but for the moments it's on screen, it's an unforgettable ride.

Familiarized with the Totoros, the sisters greatest adventure comes in the field of agriculture. Having planted some acorns in the garden, the troupe of children and forest spirits dance around them, willing them to grow. Joe Hisaishi's ethereal score swells and the screen becomes enveloped with shooting greenery; it is Miyazaki's vision of environmental harmony at a grand scale, and it's breathtaking.

The final shot of the film is of the Totoros, atop the camphor tree, watching out with those wide eyes. It is reassuring to see them there, reminding us that whatever troubles we might face, even if we face them stoically, there is a big, furry ball of goodness who can help in the hardest of times. Whether that's by helping to find a missing child, or just by giving that child a nice place to nap. King Totoro still holds his umbrella, gifted by Satsuki, and we've got Totoro, a gift to us.

# GRAVE OF THE FIREFLIES (HOTARU NO HAKA, 1988)

## TAKAHATA'S TRAGIC TEAR-JERKER

DIRECTED BY: ISAO TAKAHATA
WRITTEN BY: ISAO TAKAHATA
LENGTH: 1HR 29MIN
RELEASE DATE (JAPAN): 16 APRIL 1988

WHEN IT COMES TO STUDIO GHIBLI'S INTERNATIONAL REPUTATION, ACCESS AFFECTS EVERYTHING. THANKS TO GLOBAL DISTRIBUTION, HAYAO MIYAZAKI'S WORLD-CONQUERING FANTASIES FROM *MY NEIGHBOUR TOTORO* TO *SPIRITED AWAY* HAVE COME TO EPITOMIZE GHIBLI, BUT HIS FILMS ONLY FORM PART OF THE STORY, AND IT HAS BEEN OUR GOAL AS GHIBLIOTHEQUE TO CELEBRATE THE FULL OUTPUT OF THE STUDIO, NOT LEAST THE WORK OF THE ENIGMATIC, ALMOST MYTHIC GHIBLI CO-FOUNDER, ISAO TAKAHATA – AFFECTIONATELY KNOWN AS "PAKU-SAN", WHICH ROUGHLY TRANSLATES AS "MR MUNCH".

Miyazaki himself explains that the origin of the nickname was Takahata's routine tardiness: he would often oversleep and rush to work, eating his breakfast as he arrived at the Studio.

Takahata's five features at Studio Ghibli have all, slowly, become available internationally, but by the 1980s he was already an influential filmmaker. Working steadily for Toei Animation in the 1960s, his ambitious 1968 directorial debut *Little Norse Prince* (*Horus: Prince of the Sun* in the US) was a box-office failure, but a key landmark for Japanese animation. It was also the first major collaboration with Hayao Miyazaki, then a junior Toei employee who worked his way up to providing key animation for the film.

Both with Miyazaki and solo, Takahata directed projects ranging from the features *Panda! Go Panda!, Chie the Brat* and *Gauche the Cellist*, to a clutch of TV series under the

**Above:** A cause for reflection. Setsuko sees herself in the water.

**Opposite:** Setsuko, one of the film's young protagonists, and cause of many tears from film fans worldwide.

*World Masterpiece Theater* umbrella, such as *Heidi, Girl of the Alps, Anne of Green Gables* and *3000 Leagues in Search of Mother*, which would inspire many of the young animators who would eventually work for Ghibli.

The majority of these series and features are currently out of circulation in the UK and US, if they were even released there in the first place. In the English-speaking (and reading) world, there's still so much to learn about Takahata and his work. Alex Dudok de Wit's compact but exhaustively researched BFI Film Classics book on *Grave of the Fireflies*, published in 2021, was by our measure at least – the first piece of widely available, in-depth critical writing on Takahata in English. It lifts the lid on a film, and filmmaker, often misunderstood or underrepresented. One key fact that Dudok de Wit stresses is that, despite his status as a "co-founder" of Studio Ghibli, Takahata refused to add his seal to the official documents at the signing ceremony in June 1985. He instead asked Suzuki if there was such a role as "playwright in residence".

Takahata was instrumental in the foundation of Ghibli in one very specific way, though. After the smash hit of *Nausicaä of the Valley of the Wind*, Miyazaki invested the profits into a mooted project to be directed by Takahata, set in the town of Yanagawa. Takahata instead made *The Story of Yanagawa's Canals*, a nearly three-hour, almost entirely live-action documentary about the region's canal system, its place in the fabric of local life and its ongoing preservation. Producer Toshio Suzuki would later say that Miyazaki's first Ghibli feature, *Laputa: Castle in the Sky*, was made just to recoup the money lost from Takahata's indulgence.

How do you even attempt to describe and distinguish

between idiosyncratic geniuses? When I find myself in times of trouble, I turn to the Beatles and their superficial, yet super-functional framework for pigeonholing pop-culture personalities. Thus, if Hayao Miyazaki is Studio Ghibli's answer to Paul McCartney – a family-friendly dream weaver beloved by millions; a multi-talented master of crafts who, frankly, could play all the parts himself if he had time and energy – then Isao Takahata is John Lennon with a sprinkle of George Harrison: an iconoclast pushing against the boundaries of his chosen medium, a visionary creator happy to work in collaboration with others, a storyteller who often tackles complex topics and themes that are much harder to swallow. As Miyazaki's films became more homogeneous in look and style during the Ghibli era, Takahata's became more innovative, varied and unpredictable, with commercial viability often an afterthought.

At the risk of stretching an already tenuous analogy past breaking point, producer Toshio Suzuki is every "fifth Beatle" mixed into one: a key creative partner, studio mastermind and an unwavering enabler for his fellow geniuses. The idea for Takahata's first animated feature for Ghibli came from Suzuki, who suggested they adapt Akiyuki Nosaka's 1967 semi-autobiographical short story *Grave of the Fireflies*. Shinchosha, the publishers of the story, were keen to enter the film industry and so would fund the production and play a key role in Suzuki's masterplan to get two Ghibli features off the ground, as covered in the previous chapter on *My Neighbour Totoro*.

Unlike Miyazaki, Takahata wasn't an animator by profession, so the key creative personnel on his projects are even more crucial to the finished work. For *Fireflies*, Takahata had star Ghibli animator Yoshifumi Kondō on board as animation director and character designer (after both Takahata and Miyazaki both requested Kondō for their features, Suzuki had to step in to resolve the impasse), Yoshiyuki Momose as assistant animation director and concept artist, and industry veteran Michiyo Yasuda as colour designer, continuing a relationship first formed on *Little Norse Prince/Horus: Prince of the Sun*.

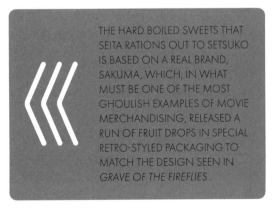

THE HARD BOILED SWEETS THAT SEITA RATIONS OUT TO SETSUKO IS BASED ON A REAL BRAND, SAKUMA, WHICH, IN WHAT MUST BE ONE OF THE MOST GHOULISH EXAMPLES OF MOVIE MERCHANDISING, RELEASED A RUN OF FRUIT DROPS IN SPECIAL RETRO-STYLED PACKAGING TO MATCH THE DESIGN SEEN IN *GRAVE OF THE FIREFLIES*.

**Above:** Setsuko joyfully watches the fireflies, her wide smile a contrasting reminder of the tragedy at the heart of the film.

A crack team, perhaps, but the production went far from smoothly. Miyazaki once characterized Takahata as having "descended from a giant sloth", in part in reference to the director's relationship with deadlines. A rigorous and extensive research process – including consulting copious reference materials, scouting story locations, even visiting a nursery to observe the movement and personalities of four-year-old girls – resulted in the production falling behind schedule. Takahata asked for an extension, but the April 1988 opening date wouldn't budge, culminating in a reputation-ruining release of an unfinished film.

The tonal whiplash of the proposed double billing of *My Neighbour Totoro* and *Grave of the Fireflies*, while a genius move for financing, baffled programmers and cinema audiences alike. It's a question still guaranteed to kickstart conversation among Ghibli fans: which film would you watch first, the uplifting adventure featuring a cuddly forest creature, or the devastating account of children fighting for survival in the dying days of the war?

The double bill continued a downward slide in ticket sales for the nascent Studio, just 450,000 after 775,000 for *Castle in the Sky*, itself down from the 915,000 attendance for *Nausicaä*. In the long term, though, *Grave of the Fireflies* would become one of Studio Ghibli's most lauded films in a variety of distinct circles: as animation, as a war film and as a day-ruining weepie.

It holds a special position in the Ghibli library that is perhaps perfectly fitting for Takahata: by consensus one of the Studio's greatest films, undoubtedly, but one that stands slightly apart. This is quite literally so when it comes to distribution. A quirk of the financing deal with Shinchosha has resulted in *Grave of the Fireflies* having different distributors to the bulk of the Studio Ghibli library in certain territories. And so, when the landmark streaming acquisitions were announced in 2020 by Netflix and

**Above:** *Grave of the Fireflies* now stands as one of the defining masterworks in the long and distinguished career of director Isao Takahata, seen here during a press interview in 1996.

**Opposite:** Seita, with Setsuko tied to his back, caught in the shocking firebombing. One of Ghibli's most devastating depictions of destruction.

HBO Max, the absence of *Grave of the Fireflies* was notable – but perhaps, given everything we know of Takahata, his work and his reluctance to play along, it was wholly appropriate.

AS WELL AS BEING A MAJOR CHAMPION FOR HAYAO MIYAZAKI, RENOWNED AMERICAN FILM CRITIC ROGER EBERT ALSO PRAISED ISAO TAKAHATA'S WORK, CALLING THE FILM "AN EMOTIONAL EXPERIENCE SO POWERFUL THAT IT FORCES A RETHINKING OF ANIMATION... *GRAVE OF THE FIREFLIES* IS A POWERFUL DRAMATIC FILM THAT HAPPENS TO BE ANIMATED."

## REVIEW: GRAVE OF THE FIREFLIES

Most Ghibli fans will probably tell you that this is up there with the studio's finest work, perhaps their greatest. They're also pretty likely to tell you that they'll never watch it again. *Grave of the Fireflies* is an incredible work of art, the animation as shatteringly powerful as the story. It's also one of the saddest films ever made.

If the first moments of a film feature a starving teenager telling you about the night he died, it's probably quite clear you're heading for an emotional time. Although it might be traumatic, unapologetic and firmly rooted in the realities of humankind – with ideological explorations of nature and warfare, as well as the occasional spiritual train ride – it is every bit a Ghibli film as some of their more far-flung, fantastical counterparts.

*Grave of the Fireflies* reveals how the teenage Seita and his younger sister Setsuko briefly live through the horrors and aftermath of World War II, navigating the destruction of the incendiary bombings of Kobe, before setting up their own life in an abandoned shelter, until they can survive no longer. Told through flashback after Seita perishes, the film is framed by the united spirits of the siblings, glazed in a copper hue, taking a train journey through their memories. There is a silent joy in these sequences that's underscored by utter tragedy; they are the most tranquil moments of these children's lives and they only come at their death. It's this balance between joy and sorrow that makes the film so upsetting, if it were all death and destruction, it would not be such despairing viewing; it is the moments where the children are allowed to be children that make it so. The horrors of war might help fill the well of tears here, but it's the joy of life that makes it overflow.

Detail is essential in Isao Takahata's films. That is not to say that they are consistently detailed though; the frames of his films may not always be hyper-realized documents of reality, but through his own more expressionist vision, they showcase reality as it is felt. Later in his career with *My Neighbours the Yamadas* and *The Tale of the Princess Kaguya* he would push his craft of imagery to only its most essential elements, and those ideas can be felt in *Grave of the Fireflies*.

The opening fifteen minutes of the film feel more akin to the plucky visions of Steven Spielberg's slightly younger-skewing wartime fares, such as *Empire of the Sun* or *War Horse*, but a shot of the children's dead mother's decaying face soon removes any comparison to the perennial Hollywood crowd-pleaser. The image is grotesque, the rough ridges of dry bandages against bloodied and burnt skin stick and itch; it lingers long on screen and even longer in the mind. This is soon followed by an image of Seita and Satsuke in the grounds of a bombed-out hospital, the horizon obliterated into fragments of a city, the sky, ground and children's faces all absorbed into the mono-colour palette of the fallout. This is Takahata's detailing, in one moment focusing so acutely on something it seems like documentary, and in another, removing the details to strip back the image but maintain its rawest emotion.

It is not just in the visuals that this stark evocation is produced, the sound is similarly powerful in its selective reproduction. Despite all of the possible sensory stimulation of a scene on a beach, the audio is localized to the incoming threat of a fleet of B-29 planes breaking through the clouds. Later as Satsuke sucks on a marble, thinking it's candy because her hunger is so great, it clicks and clacks around her teeth like a rock hitting the edges of a cave. Some films might want to be overwhelming to reflect the wartime experience (*Saving Private Ryan* would be our Spielberg for that particular technique), but rather than a scattered approach, *Grave of the Fireflies* is focused in its use of sound and vision. Rather than create an all-encompassing time capsule, the film heightens specifics, reflecting a concentrated memory of trauma.

Seita and Satsuke's plight is gruelling but inspiring, their hope and pragmatism a light to cling to as the world around them crumbles into physical, economic and emotional disrepair. They are the fireflies of the title, burning beautifully and bright, all too briefly. After Satsuke admires some fireflies outside in the wild, the siblings capture some, trapping them in a net so they can light their shelter, only to wake up and find that they have died. It is one of the most evocative pieces of imagery in Ghibli's work and as well as the metaphorical connection to Seita and Satsuke, it explores the studio's ongoing relationship to nature and industrialism. Fireflies are a stunning and delicate creation of the natural world, and when the film lingers on their drifting flight through the night sky, this is recognized. But as they continue to glide their lights begin to mesh with those of the firebombs raining down on the city (an image used in the film's poster), and in the shadows of the B-29 the beauty of a natural organism is bastardized and destroyed; the romantic image of lights in the sky that Satsuke loved, stolen by warfare.

In the final moments of the film, now freed from their torturous experience of war and their purgatorial commute through the memory of it, Seita and Satsuke rest, sitting in a swarm of fireflies that drift into the sky of the city. It might not be noticeable on the first watch, particularly as most viewers will be watching through a film of tears, but it's modern-day Kobe that they float above. The copper hue of the past shares the frame with the crisp blues of modernity, the fireflies floating between the two; a gentle and beautiful reminder of the city's tragedy.

**Opposite:** The Japanese-language poster for *Grave of the Fireflies.*

# KIKI'S DELIVERY SERVICE (MAJO NO TAKKYŪBIN, 1989)

## THE LITTLE WITCH WHO SAVED STUDIO GHIBLI

DIRECTED BY: HAYAO MIYAZAKI
WRITTEN BY: HAYAO MIYAZAKI
LENGTH: 1HR 43MIN
RELEASE DATE (JAPAN): 29 JULY 1989

THREE FILMS INTO ITS LIFE, STUDIO GHIBLI WAS IN A SLUMP. *LAPUTA: CASTLE IN THE SKY*, *MY NEIGHBOUR TOTORO* AND *GRAVE OF THE FIREFLIES* HAD FAILED TO DELIVER ON THE PROMISE OF *NAUSICAÄ OF THE VALLEY OF THE WIND*, THE BLOCKBUSTER THAT INSPIRED THE FORMATION OF A STUDIO FOCUSED ON THEATRICAL, FEATURE-LENGTH FILMS.

The day after completing work on *My Neighbour Totoro*, Miyazaki started planning for his next project, an adaptation of Eiko Kadono's popular children's novel *Kiki's Delivery Service*, which follows a young witch's first footsteps into adulthood, as she leaves home, settles into a new town and finds her calling. In his directorial statement, dated April 1988, Miyazaki ruminated on the modern-day comforts that can often keep young adults in a state of arrested development:

"It is no longer appropriate to refer to leaving one's parents as a rite of passage, because all it takes today to live on one's own in society is the ability to shop at the local convenience store. The true 'independence' girls must now confront involves the far more difficult task of discovering their own talents."

Initially, Miyazaki was to take a break from directing and act solely as producer on *Kiki's Delivery Service*, with former *Sherlock Hound* writer Sunao Katabuchi set to make his debut as director, and writer Nobuyuki Isshiki on script duties. However, Miyazaki wasn't happy with the first draft of the screenplay, so he rewrote it himself, and eventually

took the reins of the project away from Katabuchi altogether, demoting him to assistant director.

Katabuchi would find success under his own steam years later, writing and directing *Princess Arete*, *Mai Mai Miracle* and the much garlanded *In This Corner of the World*. He now has a diplomatic view of his ousting from *Kiki's Delivery Service*: he'd been brought in on loan from Mushi Production to give Miyazaki a break from directing after *My Neighbour Totoro*. "However, for some reason he changed his mind and thought he could handle it," Katabuchi says. "Maybe he regained strength."

That strength would come in handy as *Kiki's Delivery Service* was by many accounts a punishing and stressful production, especially when it came to the discussions with author Eiko Kadono about Miyazaki's adaptation, which included

**Opposite:** Kiki soars above the seaside town of Koriko.

**Below:** Relaxing on a grassy hill – a recurring pastime for Ghibli's protagonists.

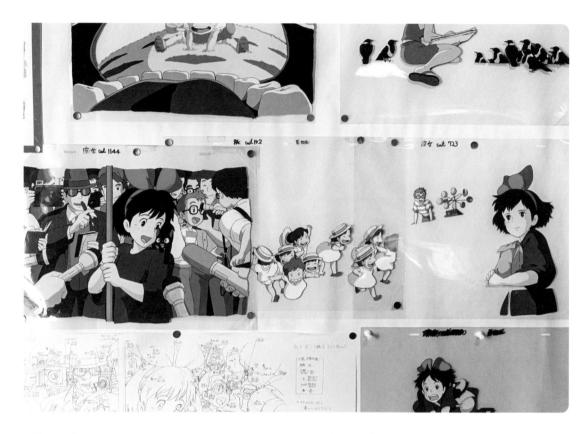

additional elements – both emotional and airborne – that weren't present in the more episodic, conflict-light original book.

Originally intended to be a 60-minute special, the film ballooned to its eventual 104-minute runtime as Miyazaki's script and storyboards took shape. The film would be in Japanese cinemas in July 1989, just over a year after Miyazaki had taken charge of the project. Gossip spread that Miyazaki was washed up and *Kiki's Delivery Service* would be his final feature as director. Working flat out for decades had taken its toll and, at 48, he was seriously considering closing up shop and retiring – starting a noble Ghibli tradition that each new Miyazaki film would, almost without exception, be touted by the filmmaker as his last.

Stepping in to smooth things over, as always, was Toshio Suzuki, who in 1989 was transferred over to Studio Ghibli from Tokuma Shoten, allowing him to dedicate himself full-time to the release of *Kiki's Delivery Service*, receiving his first individual credit on a Ghibli feature as associate producer. Frankly, he was underbilled, as this was where Suzuki's flair for marketing and advertising came to the fore. Noting the similarity between the film's title and the courier company Yamato Delivery Service, which has a prominent black cat on their logo, Suzuki brokered a deal for sponsorship and commercial tie-ins, which later helped secure a distribution deal from Toei.

In fact, Suzuki recalls that it was Toei's head of distribution predicting that *Kiki* would spell "the end" of both Ghibli and Miyazaki's career that spurred him on to ensure the film would be a hit. To that end, his primary focus was on delivering the film to its target demographic, namely young working women who would relate to Kiki's story of flying the nest and fending for herself in the face of life, work and loneliness. A stroke of inspiration came with the combination of a tagline that struck right to the heart of this complex emotional appeal – "I was feeling blue, but I'm better now" – with poster art that shows Kiki slumped at Osono's bakery counter, the weight of the world on her shoulders.

Suzuki's magic worked, and *Kiki* took flight. A runaway success, the film was the highest-grossing Japanese movie at the national box office in 1989. In fact, even with Hollywood films included, it was third, behind only *Indiana Jones and the Last Crusade* and *Rain Man*. Bigger hits were to come in the ensuing decade and beyond, but for now Ghibli was back on track, and Miyazaki finally had another hit to his name.

**Above:** Sketches and cels from *Kiki's Delivery Service*, as seen at the Ghibli Museum.

**Opposite:** The Japanese-language poster for *Kiki's Delivery Service*, downbeat but depicting perfectly the film's focus on the personal challenges our young, independent protagonist must face.

宮崎 駿 監督作品

# 魔女の宅急便

角野栄子「魔女の宅急便」(福音館書店刊)より●徳間書店・ヤマト運輸・日本テレビ放送網提携作品 ●配給／東映

## '89年夏、全国洋画系ロードショー

おちこんだりもしたけれど、私はげんきです。

It is fitting that *Kiki's Delivery Service* became the film to secure Ghibli's financial and creative stability after a rocky start. The young witch and the studio were in their adolescence, they faced hardships, but they came out more independently confident than before. The film is a warming slice of Ghibli (or herring) pie, baked with all the ingredients that make you come back to Ghibli for seconds and thirds.

It starts with a crisp blue sky. That perfect Ghibli blue. Then the wind-fluttered rolling green hills that no one else does better. It's a simple combination of land and air, but in their hands, whether it's here, in *Howl's Moving Castle*, *The Wind Rises* or *Arrietty*, a Ghibli hillside seems like Eden. Relaxing in this pristine valley is Kiki, the young witch, about to start her adventure into adulthood. Broom in hand, cat by her side, she'll learn about finding her place in the world, the importance of hard work, and she'll find adversity in personal challenges, rather than those imposed by an antagonist. She is the archetypal Ghibli protagonist.

The director's statement from Hayao Miyazaki that talks of the "true independence" that "girls must now confront", certainly fits Kiki's story of striking out by herself and starting her own courier business. It could also apply to the ferocious warrior-wolf San in *Princess Mononoke*, to Chihiro – the best bathhouse cleaner this side of the train tracks – in *Spirited Away*, or big-hearted explorer Arrietty, and quietly brave Anna in *When Marnie Was There*. Kiki's DNA runs right through so much of Ghibli's family of characters.

Kiki's world, although smaller than some of the sprawling fantasy landscapes of *Nausicaä* or *Howl's Moving Castle*, is one of Ghibli's most encompassing. Their adaptation of *Tales from Earthsea* presents an enormous world, but never finds the story to fill it. Here is the reverse, a small story that progressively finds the magic to fill its world. Kiki's journey features stunning aerial panoramas of sea and sky, and although she might be able to fly above them, the street-level comforts of her new hometown of Koriko – a bakery, a clock tower, a bustling street – are provided in just as much detail. To Kiki, there is as much adventure in the everyday workings of a community as there is whizzing through the air. There is a humming sense of life and place in Koriko, and that may well be down to the producer Toshio Suzuki. As well as mapping out the finances for Ghibli, he knew the importance of geography too. "It is one of the most important jobs of a producer to create maps," he said, "whether based on real or imaginary worlds." In his work shaping Koriko, he did both, taking the imaginary and making it real.

The interlacing of fantasy and reality is at the core of so much of Miyazaki's work; the natural and supernatural will often combine to reveal magic. Although there are no enormously fantastical creatures, there is one moment in *Kiki's Delivery Service* that captures this ethos in perhaps the most refined way of all of his films. As Kiki, our young supernatural heroine, is soaring through the sky, she joins a V-formation of geese and very briefly flies in harmony with them. It is typical of the director – who grew up sketching planes, and would go on to focus directly on aviation in *Porco Rosso* and *The Wind Rises* – that this moment happens mid-air. Through the magic of flight, however short, a harmony is found between people and their environment.

It is through togetherness, be it with birds or people, that Kiki thrives. Her independence is not fought for independently. Osono the baker is one of the first people that supports Kiki, not just by providing a roof over her head, but through the simple act of encouragement. She helps Kiki set up her delivery service, bring in customers and still has time to run a bakery – all while being in the late stages of pregnancy. Later, when Kiki's magic seems to be failing, local artist Ursula is able to offer words of support, and (as in *Spirited Away*, *Howl's Moving Castle* and *From Up on Poppy Hill*) we're shown how a good spring clean can help a cluttered mind. It's an inspirational message for anyone in the midst of a creative crisis; Kiki's skills have to be continually developed, so that the next obstacle may be overcome.

More so than the film's message of independence, garnered through communal support, is the film's emotional landing. Just as Kiki recognizes that her magic can fluctuate, she also recognizes that her feelings can as well. She is not blindly stoic, revealing that despite her great adventure, she still feels sad sometimes and that that is ok. *Kiki's Delivery Service* might inspire you, and make you feel like you can conquer Koriko, but crucially, if you feel like you can't, that's totally valid too. Sometimes just staying inside, playing with your talking cat and making pancakes can be magical as well.

PRODUCER TOSHIO SUZUKI SAID THAT "BEING ABLE TO DRAW A MAP IS ONE OF THE BASIC SKILLS ONE HAS TO LEARN IN LIFE". HERE KIKI NAVIGATES HER OWN TOWN FROM THE SKY.

# ONLY YESTERDAY
# (OMOIDE PORO PORO, 1991)

## PAINSTAKING RESEARCH
## AND RELENTLESS REALISM

DIRECTED BY: ISAO TAKAHATA
WRITTEN BY: ISAO TAKAHATA
LENGTH: 1HR 58MIN
RELEASE DATE (JAPAN): 20 JULY 1991

To his mind, there was only one filmmaker who could solve it: Takahata. It was the older filmmaker's suggestion to bring in a frame narrative, focusing on Taeko as an adult, leaving the bustle of Tokyo for a potentially life-changing vacation in the Yamagata countryside, during which her thoughts drift back to memories from her childhood.

"Miyazaki being the producer is the only reason we're here today." Takahata says in a making-of documentary shot for the release of *Only Yesterday*. "An ordinary 27-year-old? It doesn't look like a hit anime! But when Miyazaki says it'll work... somehow they're convinced."

Also on board was Toshio Suzuki, making his first appearance as a full-blown producer on a Studio Ghibli film – a role he would reprise on dozens of features over the ensuing two decades. In his memoir *Mixing Work with Pleasure*, Suzuki recalls that, while Takahata was a consummate producer, as a director he "turned out to be a pain in the neck, exercising his perfectionist tendencies to the ultimate degree."

"Paku-san [Takahata] is the one who can drive me mad the most." Miyazaki confesses in the *Only Yesterday* making-of documentary. "Having said that, he's the one I can trust the most."

That trust would be tested. Originally slated for release in 1990, the film slipped behind schedule, and it would fall to

Miyazaki to negotiate with the corporate backers to push the release to July 1991 in order to avoid rushing through a botch-job or outsourcing to inferior studios that would sacrifice the expected Ghibli quality.

Suzuki describes Takahata's two primary concerns while making *Only Yesterday* to be "painstaking research" and "relentless realism". In an uncommon move for Ghibli and animation in general, Takahata filmed reference footage of the voice actors for the adult Taeko narrative thread, so that animation director Yoshifumi Kondō and his team could give the characters realistic facial expressions, highlighting facial muscles, cheekbones and wrinkles to a depth of detail not often seen in animation.

Likewise, it's hard to imagine any other production, animation or otherwise, going to the lengths Takahata did when researching the scenes in the film involving the growing, picking and processing of safflowers. In the middle of production, Takahata, Suzuki and a group of staffers visited Yamagata,

**Opposite:** The past and present collide in Takahata's nostalgic gem, *Only Yesterday*.

**Below:** A pastoral scene from *Only Yesterday*, a result of Takahata's "painstaking research" into the safflower picking process.

私はワタシと旅にでる。

宮崎 駿プロデュース■高畑 勲監督作品

# おもひでぽろぽろ

《声の出演》今井美樹・柳葉敏郎 《主題歌》都はるみ

原作 岡本 螢/刀根夕子(徳間書店・青林堂刊) ■音楽 星 勝(徳間ジャパン) ■徳間書店・日本テレビ放送網・博報堂提携作品 ■制作 スタジオジブリ ■配給 東宝

shadowing safflower farmers and filming them for reference footage – such was the pursuit of absolute authenticity.

When it was finally released, *Only Yesterday* was a surprise smash. Like *Kiki's Delivery Service* before it, it topped the charts at the end of the year as the highest-grossing Japanese film at the domestic box office, only lagging behind Hollywood juggernauts such as *Total Recall* and *Terminator 2: Judgment Day*. Takahata had been exonerated.

But *Only Yesterday*'s international judgement day wouldn't come for over a decade. After the landmark deal that Ghibli's parent company, Tokuma Shoten, brokered with Disney for distribution of Miyazaki and Takahata's films in the US and elsewhere, *Only Yesterday* was shelved indefinitely due to "inappropriate" scenes involving discussions of menstruation.

Fortunately, according to former Ghibli executive Steve Alpert, Disney had decided against retaining digital rights for the catalogue, so with the advent of DVD, the Studio was able to reclaim the films for international distribution, and viewers in Europe, Australia and elsewhere were able to see the film

from 2006, after which *Only Yesterday* quickly became a cult favourite. It wouldn't be until 2016 that GKIDS released *Only Yesterday* in the US both in cinemas and on home video, complete with a new English-language audio track starring Daisy Ridley and Dev Patel.

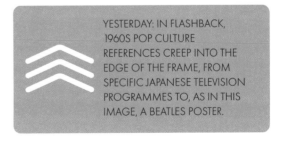

YESTERDAY: IN FLASHBACK, 1960S POP CULTURE REFERENCES CREEP INTO THE EDGE OF THE FRAME, FROM SPECIFIC JAPANESE TELEVISION PROGRAMMES TO, AS IN THIS IMAGE, A BEATLES POSTER.

**Opposite:** The Japanese-language poster for *Only Yesterday*.

In a Ghibli film, when you need to change your life you sometimes have to battle with a sublime bathhouse filled with spirits, monsters and witches, take a spiritual train journey and come out the other side altered forever. Other times you might just need a visit to the countryside. You'll still have a spiritual train ride though. Isao Takahata's *Only Yesterday* is a gentle masterwork in Ghibli's canon, one that is as transportive as Miyazaki's *Spirited Away*, with its tangible divinity found firmly in realism and memory. The story is about Taeko, a 27-year-old woman who uses a vacation from her city office job to travel and work on a rural farm, reminiscing throughout about the defining moments of her childhood. It is a simple story told with generous detail, Taeko's journey down memory lane and its surrounding fields becoming a vibrant personal and social introspection, as seemingly minor events of her youth shape her modern self.

Powerful stylistic techniques from Takahata's previous film *Grave of the Fireflies* carry over into *Only Yesterday*. In the previous film different coloured hues signified the narrative as coming from the perspective of the living or dead, here a more extreme dual aesthetic offers stirring contrast and communication between memory and the present. The crystal-sharp shape of an office building is one of the first images of the film, it is boxy, modern and almost hyper-real, with the city expanding around it to fill the frame. The realm of memory in the film, however, is vastly different. The young Taeko's world is not always full of every detail, but the ones that matter; her rounder, softly coloured world barely reaches the edge of frame, bleached by the light of memory. The established formalism of the present allows Takahata to apply anthropological, documentary detail to Taeko's rural excursion while the looser look of the past opens the door for thrilling expressionism. Separately they are brilliant worlds, and in moments of stylistic alchemy, their overlapping allows the film to reach further emotional and creative highs.

Arriving in the countryside by train, Taeko is collected by Toshio, a young organic farmer. On the drive Toshio goes into great detail about the practices of organic farming, the struggles of agriculture and modern market reforms (that might sound like it's from *Star Wars: The Phantom Menace*, but honestly, it's fascinating) before arriving at the farm. Takahata composes the workers centrally, one after the other, smiling as they look into the centre of the frame, like posed portraits from an expedition journal. In one of many extraordinary sequences from the farm, the story shifts to focus on the process of making rouge from the harvesting of safflowers. The exquisite detail pays off hugely as the nuance and skill of the workers, their collaborative plucking, squelching and grinding, forms

a rhythmic documentary elegy. Toshio considers existence to be a joint venture between humans and the earth, through Takahata's lens and in these moments it can be a perfect working relationship.

In between shifts, Taeko digs into her past, harvesting memories of food, young love, and puberty. An entertaining chapter about menstruation doesn't shy away from the occasionally cutting barbs of teenagers, while offering a refreshingly reassuring adolescent guide for people with periods. A family's excited first encounter with a pineapple becomes a confused surgical operation, followed by a cringe-inducing stand-off of disappointed chewing and a vital lesson in expectation. In the most memorable sequence from the past, Takahata continues to push the form of his world to align it with emotion, as an awkwardly pure moment of youthful romance joyfully sends Taeko climbing up invisible stairs and flying into the sky. There is expressionist clarity to the scene, the backgrounds disappearing to become a dream of pink hues, allowing Taeko and the film to soar.

There are parallels between *Only Yesterday* and that other, often forgotten, more realist Ghibli masterpiece *Whisper of the Heart*. In her present, like Shizuku, the protagonist in Yoshifumi Kondō's film that would be released a few years later, Taeko has a gap in her life that she is searching to fill through a creative passion. Neither character has a quick fix either; it is through work and dedication that their crafts and passions are honed, whether that is creative writing for Shizuku or life on the farm for Taeko. And just as following a cat who gets on a train takes Shizuku on a life-changing adventure, it is a train journey at the end of *Only Yesterday* that similarly opens up a new chapter in Taeko's life. It is a big claim, but the finale of *Only Yesterday* may be the ultimate Ghibli train scene. On a journey back to the city, after spending years apart, disconnected by memory, Taeko and her younger self reunite. Along with her school classmates, the young Taeko cheers on her older self as

she decides to alight and return to the farm and a blossoming life with Toshio. The sharp and soft worlds of the film finally fold into each other, Taeko embracing her lived experience that formed her present self, both the good and the bad memories, no longer looking at her past from a distance, but sitting alongside it. She may end up with Toshio, but having gone through a tranquil rural therapy session, *Only Yesterday* shows that the most important personal union can be with oneself.

**Opposite:** Jake, the happiest he's ever been, on discovering an *Only Yesterday* poster at Nakano Broadway, Tokyo.

ONLY YESTERDAY'S FLASHBACK SEQUENCES ARE WASHED-OUT, FADING TO WHITE AT THE EDGES, AS IF THE VERY FRAME WERE SLIPPING AWAY LIKE HALF-FORGOTTEN MEMORIES. ISAO TAKAHATA WOULD REVISIT THIS MORE MINIMALIST, EXPRESSIONISTIC STYLE IN HIS LATER FILMS *MY NEIGHBOURS THE YAMADAS* AND *THE TALE OF THE PRINCESS KAGUYA.*

# PORCO ROSSO
# (KURENAI NO BUTA, 1992)

## YOU'LL BELIEVE A PIG CAN FLY

DIRECTED BY: HAYAO MIYAZAKI
WRITTEN BY: HAYAO MIYAZAKI
LENGTH: 1HR 34MIN
RELEASE DATE (JAPAN): 18 JULY 1992

LET'S DROP THIS BOMBSHELL EARLY: HAYAO MIYAZAKI LOVES PLANES. SCENES OF FLIGHT AND AIRCRAFT BOTH FANTASY AND REAL ARE PEPPERED THROUGHOUT HIS WORK, FROM THE BUZZING "FLAPTORS" OF *CASTLE IN THE SKY*, TO THE ZEPPELIN THAT INJECTS DRAMA TO THE FINAL ACT OF *KIKI'S DELIVERY SERVICE*. HE WOULD LATER DIG DEEP INTO THE HISTORY OF AVIATION AND ENGINEERING IN *THE WIND RISES*, BUT, UNTIL THEN, THE MOST ELABORATE DISPLAY OF HIS OBSESSION WITH PLANES AND FLIGHT WAS 1992'S FLYING ACE ADVENTURE, *PORCO ROSSO*.

The roots of *Porco Rosso* lie in a series of manga stories, sketches and illustrated essays that Miyazaki contributed to the hobbyist magazine *Model Graphix* across the 1980s and into the early 1990s, often during breaks between films or while drawing the epic manga series of *Nausicaä of the Valley of the Wind*.

"The truth is that I am happiest when I am writing about stupid airplanes and tanks in magazines like *Model Graphix*," Miyazaki remarked in a 1989 interview with *Comic Box*, and it's in these short works (later collected as Hayao Miyazaki's *Daydream Data Notes*) that Miyazaki first toyed with a pig protagonist.

A mooted animation in the mid-1980s, adapted from a *Model Graphix* manga and featuring a rogue tank commander who was a pig, was shelved when Miyazaki, hard at work on *Castle in the Sky*, clashed with the younger filmmaker tasked with leading the project. Yet the pig returned, years later, in a story titled *The Age of the Flying Boat* – the difference was he was now a pig aviator, the

setting became the Adriatic Sea and the time period shifted to between World War I and World War II.

Miyazaki was happy to keep his feature films and fanciful *Model Graphix* contributions separate, but an unlikely commission to develop a 45-minute in-flight film for Japan Airlines seemed like the perfect runway for *The Age of the Flying Boat*. Miyazaki initially envisioned the project as pure, escapist entertainment, writing in his directorial memoranda from April 1991:

"*Porco Rosso* is designed to be a work that businessmen exhausted from international flights can enjoy even if their minds have been dulled from lack of oxygen. It must also be a work that boys and girls, as well as aunties, can enjoy, but we must never forget that first of all it is a cartoon movie for tired, middle-aged men whose brain cells have turned to tofu."

**Opposite:** Thumbs up. Porco Rosso, in one of Ghibli's most shareable images.

**Below:** Putting your talents to work. Porco and Fio join forces

Production continued apace, and set in motion a process that has come to define Miyazaki's approach to filmmaking: starting work on key animation before the storyboards had been completed, in other words before the ending of the film had even been written. Toshio Suzuki recalls that this "cart before the horse" method, first implemented because the production was so far behind schedule, became firmly established, prompting Miyazaki to enthusiastically remark: "It's no fun when everything has been worked out ahead of time, is it?"

One downside to this method, as becomes the case on later Ghibli projects, is that while the animators are hard at work on the completed sections of the storyboards, the plotting of the film can still change shape right up until Miyazaki lays down his pencil. This results in endings that may seem rushed or, in *Porco Rosso's* case, a 45-minute short that ended up growing into a 90-minute feature film. The in-flight movie would instead appear in cinemas.

**Above:** Prime Porco-related paraphernalia at the Ghibli Museum.

**Right:** Picture perfect. Fio and the airmen pilot a chaotic pose.

Over the course of adapting his manga into storyboards, Miyazaki had introduced additional texture inspired by his anxieties in response to news coverage of the Gulf War and the conflict in Yugoslavia – bigger, potentially unsettling themes that couldn't be further from the initial plan to present viewers with a "worry-free, stirring, uplifting world". Speaking after *Porco Rosso*'s release, he describes this shift in his worldview:

"Heading into the twenty-first century, nothing's been resolved. Everything's been dragged into the new era, so we'll just have to go on living, repeating the same stupid mistakes over and over again. That's the realization I've had."

This change in mood would mark each of his ensuing films, from *Princess Mononoke* onwards. "No matter how messy things get," he remarked, "we have no choice but to go on living... You may not like what's happening, but just accept it, and let's try to live together.

"I've realized that this is the only way forward... It's important not to fall for some cheap nihilism or for living for the moment... Be willing to take a certain amount of risk to preserve the environment... And make sure you do crazy things once in a while."

*Porco Rosso* was a huge hit in Japan in the summer of 1992, ending the year at the top of the box office, out-grossing major Hollywood films such as Disney's *Beauty and the Beast* and *Hook*. In fact, it stood, for many years, as the highest-grossing Japanese animation of all time – at least until Miyazaki's next film came along.

**Above:** Hold on tight. Porco steers one of Ghibli's most high-octane adventures.

**Opposite:** The Japanese-language poster for *Porco Rosso*.

In *Porco Rosso*, when our down-and-out hero needs a new powerful engine fitted for his crimson seaplane, the one he selects has a single word emblazoned in the metal: "Ghibli". It's not a brazen ego-stroke from the studio, the Caproni Ca.309 Ghibli was a real plane, and it flew during the same inter-war period that *Porco Rosso* is set. It's also not just an engine for the porcine pilot but one for Hayao Miyazaki as well. His heart and sketchbooks always full of aeroplane designs, *Porco Rosso* is the culmination of decades of love, and with the full production engine of Ghibli powering him, his passion could take flight.

Featuring lush blues and greens, a European setting and focus on flight, it seems like classic Ghibli fare, but with fresh, dry humour and a zinging script, tonally it remains unique in the studio's catalogue. It has the spirit of a lively international capering adventure that evokes Hergé's *Tintin* and a swaggering competence for action that could rival the *Indiana Jones* films. It may not be one of the most popular Miyazaki films, but *Porco Rosso* is a soaring achievement in animation and story for Ghibli.

The opening credits of the film, styled like telegrams being punched on screen, may not immediately rank it alongside the great weathered tapestry that opens *Nausicaä* or the soothing, block colour seascape titles of *Ponyo*, but they fling the viewer into the world of the film. In a telegram, where words are at a premium, you need to know where and when you are and that "the name of the hero of our story is Crimson Pig". Streaming across the screen, the words are slammed on

the keys in ten different languages, urgently typed from the past to call us into adventure. Ghibli wants passengers the world over to get on board with them as quickly as possible, it's going to be an incredible flight.

Porco himself is not a straight-laced hero, more like a Han Solo (or is that Ham Solo), who knows the right thing to do, even if he doesn't fly at the chance to do it. *Porco Rosso* is Miyazaki's most quippy script, and Porco himself is one of the studio's most outwardly comedic creations, his tongue as sharp as his flying skills. In one of Ghibli's most quoted lines, after refusing to rejoin the Italian air force, he says that he'd "rather be a pig, than a fascist".

Porco's first task in the film is to rescue a group of young girls who have been kidnapped by sky pirates, something he must somehow steel himself to do, instead of reading *Cinema* magazine and snoozing away in his picturesque Adriatic island cove hideout. This first rescue instantly shows the years of work Miyazaki had unconsciously put into the film by persistently drawing planes. In a live action film, Porco's Savoia S.21 seaplane would fly past the camera at whiplash-inducing speed; in animation, it can remain in the frame and flash all its best angles, from its perfectly round red nose, to its tricolour tail. Like all the flight sequences in *Porco Rosso*, it is not just beautifully drawn, but perfectly choreographed. Porco and the pirates dance through sea and sky, trading daring manoeuvres and morse-code barbs, in an elegant and thrilling bout to open the film's proceedings. Aside from the action, the young girls are revealed to be far from damsels in

**Above:** The pencil moustached Donald Curtis, voiced by Akio Otsuka in the original and a dastardly Cary Elwes in the English language version.

**Opposite:** On your left. Porco mid-dogfight.

distress – following in the spirit of Mei and Satsuki screaming in delight at their haunted house in *My Neighbour Totoro* – the kidnapped girls are feisty, funny and totally nonplussed by their captors. They are also the first, but by no means the last, female characters to pleasantly steal the film's flightpath away from the crimson pig.

After Porco's plane is almost destroyed by the film's baddy Curtis (first name Donald – a gun-toting idiot celebrity with dreams of becoming the American president...), he takes it to Milan and his mechanic Piccolo. Here, Porco is introduced to Piccolo's granddaughter Fio (who seems to have been leafing through *Nausicaä*'s look-book), and her team of female mechanics, brought in to replace the men who had left to find work during the depression. This partially reflects what was happening in the studio at the time; Toshio Suzuki had brought in female staff to replace the men who were working on *Only Yesterday*, and so they became the heroic mechanics in *Porco Rosso* as well. In the workshop, the film settles into a satisfying rhythm of message and style.

Throughout his works, whether it is assembling a meal, or cleaning a bathhouse, Miyazaki finds huge gratification in

a job well done, and that is true again with the rebuilding of Porco's plane. From the first sketches, to the wood frame construction, to the careful final lowering of the engine, it is a precise and graceful process – as we'd expect from a director with such strong aviation affection. It is an exercise in patience, Porco won't stump up his cash to have the job done quickly, he'll do it to have the job done well. In these moments, Miyazaki's great loves of aviation and animation become perfectly entwined. The staff at the workshop are a mirror of the staff at Ghibli, and their work is too. Like Ghibli's animation, the Piccolo team might not be the fastest, but they are the best.

Ghibli's animators work wonders throughout the film, whether that is crafting blistering action or quiet solitude, but one moment stands above the rest and above any other moment in all of Ghibli's entire library. Recalling the memory of a swarming dogfight, after Porco's squadron are felled, he flies above the clouds and skims along their cream-like top. His fallen comrades appear beside him and tranquilly climb higher, towards a glittering field of white that is belted around the crisp blue sky. It looks like the milky way but as the pilots silently climb higher still, it is revealed that this celestial ribbon is in fact made of aeroplanes, as they are destroyed on earth, they then ride above the clouds to join this sublime funeral march. To Miyazaki the aeroplanes are as soulful as their pilots, both carried into this beyond, an omnipresent angelic ring around our planet, the twinkle of heavenly aeroplane and the cosmic body becoming one. It is, and the film is, Ghibli at its awe-inspiring best.

# OCEAN WAVES
# (UMI GA KIKOERU, 1993)

## STUDIO GHIBLI:
## THE NEXT GENERATION

DIRECTED BY: TOMOMI MOCHIZUKI
WRITTEN BY: KEIKO NIWA
LENGTH: 1HR 12MIN
RELEASE DATE (JAPAN): 5 MAY 1993 (TV)

BY 1993, STUDIO GHIBLI WAS AT PEAK PRODUCTIVITY. *KIKI'S DELIVERY SERVICE, ONLY YESTERDAY* AND *PORCO ROSSO* WERE THE HIGHEST-GROSSING JAPANESE FILMS AT THE NATIONAL BOX OFFICE IN THEIR RESPECTIVE YEARS, BUT BOTH HAYAO MIYAZAKI AND ISAO TAKAHATA WERE NOW IN THEIR FIFTIES; WHERE WOULD THE STUDIO GO IF ONE, OR BOTH, RETIRED?

Adapted from the novella by Saeko Himuro, *Ocean Waves* was conceived as the first of many solutions to this perennial problem: a project for Ghibli's younger staff members, giving those in their twenties or thirties who had gained invaluable experience working on films for Miyazaki and Takahata the space and opportunity to stretch their creative muscles on a project of their own.

Crucially, this would make *Ocean Waves* the first Ghibli project not to be directed by either of their founding filmmakers. Instead, directorial duties fell to 34-year-old Tomomi Mochizuki, who even at that relatively young age had notched up an impressive CV directing anime TV series through the 1980s, including the anime adaptation of Rumiko Takahashi's popular shape-shifting fantasy series *Ranma ½*.

Mochizuki was a newcomer to Ghibli, but he was backed up by a stellar crew of Studio stalwarts and rising stars. Two of the Studio's prize animators, Yoshifumi Kondō and Katsuya Kondō, were on board, with the latter providing character designs based on their illustrations from the novella's serialization in the Ghibli-adjacent anime periodical *Animage*, while relative newcomer Masashi Ando, who would have an enviable career as character designer and animation director both for Ghibli (*Princess Mononoke, Spirited Away*) and elsewhere (*Paprika, Your Name*), provided key animation. Notable, too, is the first Ghibli credit for screenwriter Keiko Niwa, who would work again with the studio over a decade later on a run of films including *Tales from Earthsea, Arrietty, From Up on Poppy Hill,*

**Above:** The train station. A pivotal location for many Studio Ghibli films.

**Opposite:** Taku and Yutaka, two sides of the *Ocean Waves* love triangle.

*When Marnie Was There* and *Earwig and the Witch*.

The original plan was for *Ocean Waves* to be a quick, cheap but good quality Ghibli production, but, as is often the Ghibli way, the production reportedly blew its deadlines and went over budget, giving Mochizuki a stress-induced ulcer and driving him away from any further collaborations with the Studio. Eventually, *Ocean Waves* was broadcast on Nippon TV in May 1993, and its status as a "TV movie", alongside Ghibli's imposing theatrical catalogue, has given it an uphill struggle for recognition. At time of writing, it is the only feature-length Studio Ghibli film not to have an English-language dub, and while it was included in the distribution deal struck with Disney in the 1990s, *Ocean Waves* wasn't released in the US until 2016, when GKIDS gave it a limited theatrical run, followed by a Blu-ray release in 2017. (A UK DVD, courtesy of Optimum Releasing, had already been released in the UK in 2010.)

If there could be such a thing as a "hidden gem" in Ghibli's catalogue, *Ocean Waves* certainly fits the bill, and out of the entire library, it might be the feature that has benefited most from the landmark deals that brought the Studio's work to the streaming services Netflix and HBO Max, which allowed scores of new fans worldwide to discover this curio and imbue it with new life, relevance and meaning.

It's a shame that its televisual origin has led *Ocean Waves* to become the least well-known Ghibli, as there are certainly other works of theirs that are more deserving of sinking to that fate. *Ocean Waves* is not a brilliant film, but it should be revered more in the Ghibli canon, because it is almost a brilliant one.

Released in between Ghibli's other romances, *Only Yesterday* and *Whisper of the Heart*, *Ocean Waves* feels pulled by the direction of both in some ways. The varying time periods and dappled, softly filled frames feel like a hangover from Takahata's film, whilst the heightened emotions and romantic gestures of adolescence would be more keenly observed in Yoshifumi Kondō's. It is a brief 76 minutes, and in that time no character is realized enough to provoke much empathy and, as the credits roll, this nostalgic piece certainly makes you think of what might have been.

The opening moments place us in recognizable Ghibli territory. There is a train station, an aeroplane and a rich blue sky; then there is one of the boldest examples of editing that the studio has ever produced. As young urbanite Taku Morisaki remembers his high school years, great white edges fill the sides of the screen, a partially recollected thumbnail image of Kōchi Castle in the centre. A moment later, a new slightly larger image takes its place, as Taku remembers working in a kitchen at the time the story began. Then, Kōchi Castle again, filling the screen, the full picture restored. It reflects memory through a hybrid of sensory and filmic technique and is used throughout the film. Memories of sense – the sound of a kitchen, rolling bike wheels on tarmac, a slap to the face – are combined with an establishing location shot, like shards of a dream, placed back together.

Taku's flight down memory lane focuses on a love triangle between himself, his friend Yutaka and the new girl at school Rikako; it is within this triangle the film gets lost. Rikako is a liar and thief, and while the boys' feelings could be attributed to misguided adolescent romance, it's hard to empathize with them, especially as the film normalizes the PE lesson leering of teenage boys, and the purchasing of unauthorized candid photography. It's not a healthy relationship and is hard to care for when the true romance of the film is right in front of them: each other.

The clearest loving bond is between the two boys. Taku talks about people not being able to "see [Yutaka's] real value", how much of a "good guy" he is, even asking about him during conversations with Rikako. When Yutaka asks if he'd like to go for a walk, the screen cuts to burning embers of a fire; and when the titular waves (or "sea") arrive, they are lit by a pastel sunset, the water glistening, lapping against a pier where the two boys stand and share a conversation more emotionally intimate than ever before. It is without question, the most romantic moment of the film. Then, in the finale, just as the film is on the cusp of being an impressively transgressive work for Ghibli, Taku declares that he is of course in love with Rikako. Ah, what might have been.

STUDY BREAK: *OCEAN WAVES* WAS THE FIRST GHIBLI FILM NOT DIRECTED BY ISAO TAKAHATA OR HAYAO MIYAZAKI, INSTEAD, THIS TV MOVIE WAS HANDLED BY TOMOMI MOCHIZUKI. GHIBLI'S FEATURE FILM WORK WOULD STICK TO BIG SCREEN RELEASES UNTIL 2020, WHEN GORO MIYAZAKI'S *EARWIG AND THE WITCH* MADE ITS TV DEBUT.

**Opposite:** The English-language poster for *Ocean Waves*.

FROM THE LEGENDARY STUDIO GHIBLI

# OCEAN

# WAVES

A TOMOMI MOCHIZUKI FILM

DIRECTOR TOSHIO SUZUKI · SEIJI OKUDA MUSIC BY SAEKO HIMURO PRODUCED BY SCREENPLAY BY KAORI NAKAMURA MUSIC BY SHIGERU NAGATA EXECUTIVE BY YOKO SAKAMOTO
TOKUMA SHOTEN · NIPPON TELEVISION NETWORK AND STUDIO GHIBLI PRESENT THE FUTURE PRODUCERS OF STUDIO GHIBLI PRODUCES "OCEAN WAVES" DIRECTED BY NOZOMU TAKAHASHI DIRECTED BY TOMOMI MOCHIZUKI
© 1993 SAEKO HIMURO · STUDIO GHIBLI · N

**COMING SOON**

# POM POKO (HEISEI TANUKI GASSEN PONPOKO, 1994)

## A BALLS-OUT ENVIRONMENTALIST PARABLE

DIRECTED BY: ISAO TAKAHATA
WRITTEN BY: ISAO TAKAHATA
LENGTH: 1HR 59MIN
RELEASE DATE (JAPAN): 16 JULY 1994

AFTER THE SUCCESS OF *PORCO ROSSO*, THE SKY WAS THE LIMIT. STUDIO GHIBLI'S NEXT PRODUCTION WOULD BE DIRECTED BY ISAO TAKAHATA, BACKED BY THE MANY OF THE SAME YOUNG STAFF MEMBERS WHO WORKED ON *ONLY YESTERDAY*, BUT THE INITIAL IDEA FOR A FILM ABOUT TANUKI, JAPAN'S NATIVE RACCOON DOGS, REPORTEDLY CAME FROM HAYAO MIYAZAKI, WHO THOUGHT IT WOULD BE A LOGICAL NEXT STEP AFTER AN ANIMATED ADVENTURE ABOUT AN ANTHROPOMORPHIC PIG.

Takahata wrote the screenplay himself, crafting a tonally complex, resonant work that saw encroaching urbanization bring destruction to the forest doorsteps of Tokyo's tanuki, often depicted as mythical, tricksy magical beings in folktales. In defence of their habitat, the tanuki club together, relearn age-old techniques that allow them to transform, and concoct elaborate illusions to scare off their human aggressors.

Miyazaki would serve as executive producer on the film, and the two old collaborators clashed on, of all things, the title. Something about *Heisei Tanuki Gassen Ponpoko* – literally, *Heisei-era Tanuki War Pom Poko*, shortened to simply *Pom Poko* for international release – bugged Miyazaki. Toshio Suzuki recalls that its playfulness rubbed up against Miyazaki's serious nature, the first half of the title suggesting an epic war movie, and "pom poko" being the onomatopoeic sound made when the tanuki drum on their bellies.

Suzuki, now firmly in place as Ghibli's producer and

**Opposite:** Prepare for war. Translated literally, *Pom Poko's* title in English is *Heisei-era Tanuki War Pom Poko...*
**Above:** ... However, the film's idiosyncratic tone strikes a balance between conflict and comedy.

ego-wrangler, backed Takahata, issuing a memo to the staff that explained that: "It is the title of the film, not the story, that is counterintuitive. If anything is to be shallow about the film, it should only be the title." Even with Suzuki's support, the curious title and topic, of the film proved to be a struggle when it came to promotion. "What we were afraid of," Suzuki recalls, "was being told that Ghibli had become predictable and boring."

*Pom Poko* continued Ghibli's streak of blockbuster successes, going on to become the highest-grossing Japanese film of 1994 at the domestic box office. Even with American releases included, it only lagged behind the popcorn-fuelled spectacle of *True Lies* and *Cliffhanger* in the final

tally. That a wistful, ultimately bittersweet film about what our embrace of modernity does to our collective memory of the past could duke it out with Planet Hollywood titans Arnold Schwarzenegger and Sylvester Stallone suggests something of the growing power of Ghibli in 1990s Japan.

Internationally, however, *Pom Poko* has always occupied a unique place in the Ghibli canon. Its renown back home was such that it was submitted as Japan's entry for the Academy Award for Best Foreign Language Film, and in 1995 it was awarded the top prize at the prestigious

Annecy International Animation Film Festival. Yet, *Pom Poko* didn't receive a wide-scale release in many Western territories until over a decade later.

Cultural specificity was no doubt a factor. While *Pom Poko* has its Western counterparts in the habitat-in-peril subgenre from *Watership Down* to *The Animals of Farthing Wood* (which premiered across Europe just a year before *Pom Poko's* release), Takahata's film is thick with references to Japanese mythology and pop culture, not least in the depiction of the tanuki themselves, which plays on a history of representation across animation, manga and folklore.

Viewers in the US and elsewhere simply don't have a relationship with these magical creatures, and so, as liberal localization teams have always done, they attempted to iron out the cultural differences in translation. The English-language dub's infamous substitution of "raccoon pouches" to describe the tanukis' elastic scrotums is quite telling compromise for the target family audience, but the obsessive fixation with the tanuki's testicles has also given *Pom Poko* an unlikely reputation as an untranslatable, baffling curio; something crude and wacky instead of thoughtful and poignant. Inquisitive Ghibli fans know, though, that there's much more to these tanuki than what's in their pants.

**Opposite:** The Japanese-language poster for *Pom Poko.*

> IN *POM POKO*, THE TANUKI TRANSFORM FROM ANIMALS, TO HUMANS, TO GHOULS AND EVEN INTO SOME OF GHIBLI'S OWN CHARACTERS. HERE THEY TRANSFORM INTO MANEKI-NEKO, A CAT FIGURINE BELIEVED TO BRING GOOD LUCK, SOMETHING THE CHARACTERS DESPERATELY NEED.

Studio Ghibli films can be unforgettable. Moments like Totoro's first big, gleaming smile, the firebombing of Kobe or No-Face's endless buffet will be lodged in the memory forever. Once seen, so too will a lot of *Pom Poko* as well. It is a film in which tanuki (Japanese racoon dogs) lead a flying attack on humans, using their testicles as both parachutes and cannon balls. And that's actually one of the more normal bits. Isao Takahata's film was made to surprise, to confirm that Studio Ghibli would never be predictable, and with that brief in mind he made a film that once seen, can never be forgotten.

There is a lot of testicle chat in this film. But once you've accepted that these racoon dogs can use their magical genitals to transform into devices of warfare, celebration and more, you'll realize that that's not even one of the most ambitious elements. Transformation is key here, both in the plot and the execution. Stylistically, *Pom Poko* is an enormous departure from the homely, whimsical fantasies of Ghibli past. An essayistic introduction, tracking the history of urban development in the film's setting of Tama Hills, is a beautifully realized abstract social document. Bulldozer cranes scoop into hillsides that look like bowls of green ice cream, construction vehicles chomp and scuttle around leaves like ants and the tanuki themselves, trying to survive around the destruction of their habitat, shift in animated appearance. Around humans they appear in their lifelike form, by themselves they are more anthropomorphic, and

occasionally they further transform into more cartoonish versions at particularly expressive moments. Beyond the tanuki's metamorphosis there are moments created in an 8-bit video game style and even more shocking, in live action.

It is a joy to watch Takahata's creative ambition flourish, and amazingly, *Pom Poko*'s story manages to almost contain its wild, stylistic scope. Compared to his previous Ghibli films *Grave of the Fireflies* and *Only Yesterday*, *Pom Poko* is a more episodic affair, tracking step by step the tanuki's failing defence of their forest in the face of urbanization. There is an almost documentary approach to the subject, beautifully detailed shots of acorns, fruit and blossom round out the collapsing forest's flora, while an assured voiceover tells of the tanuki's plight, as if recalled from a historical text.

One standout chapter features the tanuki using their skills in transformation to appear as humans without faces, scaring off construction workers – and viewers as well. It's one of Ghibli's most outright scary moments and although *Spirited Away* might get the attention, *Pom Poko* can claim the first iconic 'no-face' Ghibli moment. In another impressive scene, the tanuki create a spectral parade in a local street, aimed to haunt the residents; it is occasionally frightening, but perhaps disappointingly for the tanuki, surprisingly peaceful. The tanuki drift through the night taking on forms inspired by centuries-old Japanese manga and woodblock prints and, in a meta move, appear as Ghibli fan favourites like Porco Rosso and Kiki too (clearly these

are tanukis of taste). These forms may be an attempt to scare people, but audiences will also appreciate the art that comes from nature and empathize with it. It is a remarkable dream of tranquil eeriness, resonating with melancholy as well as fright; the machine of industrialism undented, the fight equally feeling like a farewell tour.

Despite their best efforts, the tanuki must vacate their forest – some learn to live as humans, some continue in their original form, living from scraps – and the green spaces of Tama Hills now more commonly found at golf clubs. Having done so at the end of *Grave of the Fireflies*, Takahata again finishes his film by panning up to a modern skyline, asking us to reflect on what destruction had to come to allow the bright lights of the city to appear. It is an affecting story, but in *Pom Poko* the cause takes precedence over character and – perhaps down to its endless pursuit of transformation – there is a barrier of personal

connection to the tanuki. Arguably this is Takahata perfectly reflecting society's colder treatment to non-human life; while we can be saddened by their circumstances, and agree that the devastation of their home is upsetting, we will just move on; this was just a document of history. However, while *Pom Poko* might lack rounded characterization, and occasionally suffers from a repetitive episodic plod, its joys are to be found in its experimentation. It is an entertaining, always surprising work of zoological study and an expressive, poetic, consistently surprising work of animation from a master of the craft.

**Opposite:** Isao Takahata's tanuki line up to take urbanisation to task.

**Below:** One moment in *Pom Poko* breaks with the Ghibli house-style completely, as the tanuki watch a cooking show that is rendered as 'live-action' footage on their TV.

# WHISPER OF THE HEART
# (MIMI O SUMASEBA, 1995)

## WHOLESOMENESS SO POWERFUL IT COULD BLOW AWAY REALITY

DIRECTED BY: YOSHIFUMI KONDŌ
WRITTEN BY: HAYAO MIYAZAKI
LENGTH: 1HR 58MIN
RELEASE DATE (JAPAN): 15 JULY 1995

A RECURRING THEME IN ANY DISCUSSION ABOUT THE STORY OF STUDIO GHIBLI IS
THAT OF SUCCESSION. HAYAO MIYAZAKI AND ISAO TAKAHATA CAST LONG SHADOWS
OVER JAPANESE ANIMATION, AND FANS AND CRITICS ALIKE LOVE TO PLAY THE GAME
OF DUBBING ANY UP-AND-COMING ANIME AUTEUR "THE NEXT MIYAZAKI". WITHIN
THE STUDIO'S OWN HISTORY, THOUGH, THE QUESTION OF HANDING OVER THE
REINS TO A YOUNGER GENERATION IS A FRAUGHT ONE – AS WE'VE SEEN ALREADY
IN THIS BOOK, AND WILL AGAIN IN LATER CHAPTERS. THAT SAID, IF THERE WAS ONE
FILMMAKER WHO SEEMED DESTINED TO CONTINUE IN THE FOOTSTEPS OF BOTH
MIYAZAKI AND TAKAHATA, IT WAS YOSHIFUMI KONDŌ.

Born in 1950, Kondō was nine and fifteen years younger than
Miyazaki and Takahata respectively, yet worked with them
consistently from the early 1970s onwards, as key animator,
character designer and animation director on anime series
ranging from *Lupin III* and *Sherlock Hound* to *Anne of Green
Gables* and *Future Boy Conan*. When he joined Ghibli, Kondō
quickly became one of the Studio's star animators, and would
be traded back and forth between the two directors' projects,
contributing to *Grave of the Fireflies*, *Kiki's Delivery Service*,
*Only Yesterday*, *Porco Rosso* and *Pom Poko*.

Miyazaki later confessed that he felt that he and Kondō
never quite clicked, and he thought that Kondō's best work
for Ghibli could be seen in his collaborations with Takahata.
That feeling might have been part of the inspiration behind
*Whisper of the Heart*, a feature project Miyazaki developed,

**Above:** This shrine actually exists in real life. See page 91 for
Michael and Jake in the same spot that Shizuku and Sugimura are
sitting in here.
**Opposite:** Country Roads: watching *Whisper of the Heart* is a
sure-fire way to have John Denver's classic country song stuck in
your head for weeks.

storyboarded and scripted as the perfect launchpad for the
animator's first foray into directing.

*Whisper of the Heart* would be adapted from Aoi Hiiragi's
manga series of the same name. It is a warm, romantic tale that
epitomizes the *shojo* genre of manga, which is aimed explicitly
at young women. Clearly thinking about how Ghibli's films
could connect with this audience, and speak to the youth of
1990s Japan, Miyazaki wrote in an October 1993 directorial
statement, titled "Why *shojo* manga now?":

"This film will represent a type of challenge issued by a bunch of middle-aged men who have lots of regrets about their own youth, to today's young people. It will attempt to stimulate a spiritual thirst, and convey the importance of yearning and aspiration to an audience that... tends to give up too easily on the idea of being the stars of their own stories."

Miyazaki's proposal concludes with an ambitious brief for the first-time director: "Wholesomeness so powerful it could blow away reality. Might not *Whisper of the Heart* be a film that accomplishes this?"

*Whisper of the Heart* developed into a hybrid project quite unlike anything Ghibli had produced before. The grounded reality of humdrum suburban Tokyo, rendered with the geographic specificity and attention to detail of a Takahata film, would melt away into flights of fancy when young protagonist Shizuku's imagination runs wild, featuring dazzling painted artwork by fine artist Naohisa Inoue. Unsurprisingly, production costs mounted, not helped by the expensive use of digital composition for these scenes.

As a result, Ghibli somewhat lost its confidence in the

**Opposite:** The Japanese poster for *Whisper of the Heart*. Note its focus on one of the film's more fantastical moments, rather than its real-world coming-of-age drama..

**Below:** The Baron. He might be a statue, but he's one of Ghibli's liveliest feline creations.

project and the prospect of a relatively unknown director, publishing marketing materials that foregrounded Miyazaki's involvement and focused on the film's fantasy elements rather than its magically mundane main story. Photographs from promotional press conferences show Miyazaki standing shoulder to shoulder with giant costumed Totoro and Porco Rosso mascots, recalling previous successes, and on release *Whisper of the Heart* would be accompanied by a new short directed by Miyazaki himself, the music video 'On Your Mark'. The implication was clear: this is a Miyazaki project, don't be mistaken.

Whether these tactics had an effect or not, *Whisper of the Heart* was a financial hit, the highest-grossing Japanese film of 1995. It wouldn't be released internationally for over a decade, but you can't fault its staying power.

Not only is the film unique in the Ghibli canon for producing a sequel (2002 spin-off *The Cat Returns*), but it continues to inspire affection in peculiar ways.

A jingle version of the song 'Take Me Home, Country Roads', which appears throughout *Whisper of the Heart*, plays on the platform at Seiseki-Sakuragaoka station as you arrive in the sleepy suburb depicted in the film. And, in perhaps Ghibli's most curious contribution to online culture, a single still frame of Shizuku sitting at her desk, deep in thought and immersed in her headphones, provided the perfect face to match the aesthetic of the "lo-fi beats to relax or study to" YouTube music channel phenomenon.

PICK OF THE LITTER. THE BARON MADE SUCH AN IMPACT IN *WHISPER OF THE HEART* THAT HE HAD THE HONOUR OF BECOMING ONE OF THE ONLY GHIBLI CHARACTERS TO MAKE IT INTO A SEQUEL, HIROYUKI MORITA'S 2002 FILM *THE CAT RETURNS*. THAT CAN HARDLY COME AS A SURPRISE THOUGH, AS GHIBLI'S LOVE OF CATS IS SO WELL DOCUMENTED, IT MAKES SENSE THAT THEY'D GIVE THE FRANCHISE TREATMENT TO A FELINE.

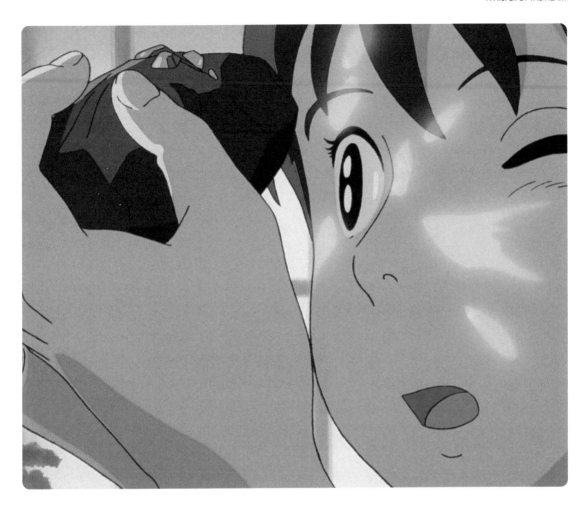

But this romance is tinged with tragedy. After *Whisper of the Heart*, Yoshifumi Kondō returned to animation duties for Miyazaki's next feature, *Princess Mononoke*, and after completing that film he suddenly died in January 1998 from what has been reported as an aortic dissection or an aneurysm.

Yoshifumi Kondō's death has come to symbolize the Japanese animation industry's culture of long hours, intense manual labour and pressure from superior team members. Suzuki would later lay the blame on Takahata and his exacting standards, recalling a meeting with Kondō during the production of *Whisper of the Heart* where the director, in tears, confided in the producer "Takahata-san tried to kill me. When I think of him, even now my body starts to shake."

At his funeral, both of his mentors delivered eulogies. Takahata called Kondō a rare talent, saying "I am sure that your work will continue to live, be loved by people, and influence people." Miyazaki spoke of the rift between the two

**Above:** To Hayao Miyazaki, our talents are uncut gems that must be worked at over time.

**Previous spread:** A young girl, a cat, a train and an adventure. Is this the quintessential Studio Ghibli image?

**Opposite:** As well as voicing Donald Curtis in *Porco Rosso*, Cary Elwes played the Baron in the English language version of *Whisper of the Heart*, and reprised the role for *The Cat Returns*.

men caused by their differing temperaments, which he felt was finally resolved with *Whisper of the Heart*.

"When he directed *Whisper of the Heart*, I felt that I finally kept the promise I made a long time ago... Although it has changed in its form as the time went by, *Whisper of the Heart* was definitely the work which we, in our twenties and thirties, had wanted to make someday."

"He often irritated me with his stubbornness," Miyazaki said. "He was the kind of person who patiently waits for the snow to melt. But this time, he has gone before me."

When you think of Ghibli's magical worlds there's a good chance there will be valleys of perfect emerald grass caught in a breeze, inventive flying machines in the sky above, and wherever you turn there are more colourful characters than in the Mos Eisley cantina. One might not instantly think of the cramped city suburb that *Whisper of the Heart* is set in as comparable to a floating city or a magical forest, but follow its sleepy winding concrete roads and the destination is one of Ghibli's most magical worlds: the real world.

Seiseki-Sakuragaoka in Tama (in the west of Tokyo and also the setting of Isao Takahata's environmentalist parable *Pom Poko*) here plays host to estranged high school students Shizuku and Seiji. In an act of passionate and stifled romance that only comes with adolescence, both are taking out the same books from the library, noticing the same names on the check out cards and unknowingly falling deeply in love with one another. It's a distanced will-they-or-won't-they that rivals *The Shop Around the Corner* and *Sleepless in Seattle* and like many a good romance before it, the setting surrounding the pair is a character in itself.

The film opens with a shot of the suburb at night, the lights

of activity sketch out the shape of the town while the beams of trains glide through it, the speckled, vibrant light recalling luminescent ocean highways in a deep blue city skyline. The streets are filled with energy, there are few static characters or vehicles, director Yoshifumi Kondō choosing instead to animate a huge amount of the backgrounds, giving the city and the story life. It is these seemingly simpler choices that create the unique transportive quality of *Whisper of the Heart*. Whether it is clothes drying in the wind that flicker over a scene, or a character grabbing rice from the cooker in the background, the details integrate us into Shizuku and Seiji's world, ingratiating them to us through our commonly realized reality.

Whilst Miyazaki and Takahata's directorial efforts may commonly enchant their films with details of nature, like a flower blooming or a bird singing, Kondō focuses more on simple human contact. A quiet time shared together in a library, the touching of hands, the slurp of noodles and the joy of singing John Denver are lingered on. Kondō is entranced as much by these gestures as anything more mystic; in *Whisper of the Heart* the rhythms of human existence present their own magic.

Not content with just being a sweeping romance and an

enrapturing tactile vision of Japan, *Whisper of the Heart* also uses Seiji and Shizuku's individual creative passions – violin making and writing respectively – to explore the nature of craft and storytelling itself. In a less interesting, more exceptionalist telling of this story Seiji would be the "chosen one" of violin making, making a Stradivarius rival in one fell chisel swoop; Shizuku, after a moment of fragility, would write a bestseller instantly. That's not what happens. When Shizuku follows a cat (this is Ghibli, of course there's a cat) from a train, up a hairpinned hill, to an antique shop, she meets Seiji's grandfather – and the shop's owner – Shirō. Shirō compares the young couple's blossoming creativity to an uncut gem, trapped in rock, unpolished, only revealed when time and effort has been put in to unleash its real beauty. It is a lesson in patience and expectation, tragically told by a director who created perfection at the first time of asking.

The story Shizuku creates provides a brief stylistic excursion for the film, as we travel into her imagination to a stunning world designed by background artist Naohisa Inoue. Inspired by surrealism and impressionism, Inoue's world features floating islands and glowing opalescent clouds that feel like an imagined Monet period of fantasy. Bouncing across them are Shizuku and the regal Baron, an anthropomorphic genteel cat, modelled after a statue in the antique shop. This brief flourish of make-believe feels like something from a Ghibli adventure past and as such reframes the story of *Whisper of the Heart*, making us consider the work of the studio itself and their work polishing the gems to reveal the stories within – the film reflexively celebrating those stories and the people that tell them.

The very end of the film supplies a minor weak point as Shizuku and Seiji rush from being strangers to being engaged, pushing aside their gentle romance for adolescent melodrama. But the questionable proposal is alleviated by the setting, echoing the melancholic endings of *Grave of the Fireflies* and *Pom Poko*, overlooking the skyline of the city. Somehow, even though the duplicated monochrome buildings could feel like a grim urbanized labyrinth, as the sun pours over them, even suburbia is filled with magic.

**Above:** If you travel out to Seiseki-Sakuragaoka station in western Tokyo, you can retrace the steps of the characters in *Whisper of the Heart*. Here's Michael and Jake sitting at the shrine, as seen in the still from the film on page 83.

**Opposite:** Through the lens of Studio Ghibli, even a sleepy suburb looks magical.

**Below:** The Baron and Shizuku in the vibrant fantasy realm of Shizuku's own creation.

# PRINCESS MONONOKE (MONONOKE-HIME, 1997)

## "NO CUT!"

DIRECTED BY: HAYAO MIYAZAKI
WRITTEN BY: HAYAO MIYAZAKI
LENGTH: 2HR 14MIN
RELEASE DATE (JAPAN): 12 JULY 1997

AND THEN, JUST OVER A DECADE INTO GHIBLI'S LIFE AS A STUDIO, EVERYTHING CHANGED. *PRINCESS MONONOKE* HAD BEEN SIMMERING AWAY IN THE MIND OF HAYAO MIYAZAKI FOR ALMOST TWENTY YEARS, AND THE RESULTING FILM WOULD SERVE AS A TURNING POINT FOR BOTH GHIBLI AND MIYAZAKI, AT HOME AND ABROAD.

The director first proposed a riff on the *Beauty and the Beast* fairy tale in 1980, producing a series of lavish watercolour concept sketches for potential production partners. When no studios expressed interest in this story of a princess living in the forest with a savage beast called a Mononoke, Miyazaki shelved the project, but returned to the idea in the early 1990s as a potential follow-up to *Porco Rosso*.

However, now in his fifties, Miyazaki's worldview and storytelling sensibilities had considerably changed, so he and producer Toshio Suzuki took the symbolic step of republishing the original Mononoke sketches as a storybook in 1993 (eventually translated into English as *Princess Mononoke – The First Story*), wiping the slate clean for Miyazaki's fresh start working the idea into a feature.

Miyazaki was also at something of a fresh start creatively since, in 1994, he had completed his long-running manga series *Nausicaä of the Valley of the Wind*. What had started in the early 1980s as source material for a feature film then continued, growing in thematic scope and complexity, often in stark contrast to the family-friendly escapism of his more

whimsical feature films. "My work has by no means ended," Miyazaki remarked in an interview as the serialization of *Nausicaä* wrapped up. "And I'm really in a bind, because as a result I don't truly feel liberated either. I wish I could say that I've just had a heavy load lifted from my shoulders... but instead what has happened is simply that the second-most difficult work I have has just moved up in rank, replacing *Nausicaä* as the most difficult work."

That next work would be *Princess Mononoke*, and it would be marked not just by the growing complexity and ambition seen in the *Nausicaä* manga, but also the darkening mood first glimpsed in *Porco Rosso*, responding to a world plagued by post-Cold War conflict and the AIDS crisis.
In a planning memo from April 1995, Miyazaki is clearly grappling with these concerns:

**Opposite:** On target. Ashitaka finds himself stuck between multiple factions in a conflict between gods and men.

**Below:** Running with the wolves. San, the princess of the wolves, is forced to engage with the violence that's destroying her forest home.

"*Princess Mononoke* does not purport to solve the problems of the entire world. The battle between rampaging forest gods and humanity cannot end well; there can be no happy ending. Yet, even amid the hatred and slaughter, there are things worthy of life. It is possible for wonderful encounters to occur and for beautiful things to exist."

No longer a simple fairy tale, *Princess Mononoke* was now a sweeping epic, set in a mythical spin on the Muromachi period in Japanese history (between the fourteenth and sixteenth centuries) as humanity's industrial expansion into the natural world started to oust the gods of old.

To best capture this ambitious proposal, Miyazaki proposed to Toshio Suzuki that Ghibli break their then consistent pattern of producing a feature-length work every year, in order to focus more time and energy on *Princess Mononoke*. Miyazaki himself reportedly had a hand in drawing or amending almost 80,000 of the film's 140,000 cels, as well as leading the staff through what is, by many accounts, a gruelling and painstaking production. Thanks to this longer process and the costly use of computer-generated animation in certain scenes (a first for the filmmaker), the budget for the film would balloon to, by Suzuki's calculations, four times that of Miyazaki's previous film, *Porco Rosso*, and two and a half times that of *Pom Poko*, making *Mononoke* Ghibli's most expensive film to date by far. It would

need to sell 4 million tickets on release, surpassing *Pom Poko*'s 3.2 million admissions, in order to be a success.

*Princess Mononoke* was released in July 1997, debuting against Steven Spielberg's *Jurassic Park: The Lost World*. A bona fide blockbuster, it sold over 12 million tickets that summer, and quickly broke records as the highest-grossing film, domestically produced or otherwise, in Japanese cinema history, eclipsing the record long-held by *E.T. the Extra-Terrestrial*. By the end of the year, though, James Cameron's juggernaut *Titanic* would edge *Mononoke* out of the top spot, but with takings that eclipsed all Ghibli's films to date, it was clear the Studio had ascended to a new stage of cultural impact.

And the world was watching. While *Princess Mononoke* was in production, Studio Ghibli's parent company Tokuma Shoten were in negotiations with film industry titans Disney to arrange worldwide distribution of the Studio's past, current and future work.

Steve Alpert, the American executive brought in to oversee Ghibli's international operations, writes at length about this phase in Ghibli's history in his illuminating and highly

**Above:** The giant, headless forest spirit towers over the landscape, a natural disaster of man's own making.

**Opposite:** The Japanese-language poster for *Princess Mononoke*.

entertaining memoir *Sharing a House with the Never-Ending Man: 15 Years at Studio Ghibli*. In 1996, Alpert was hired by Toshio Suzuki, who believed it was time that Ghibli's films got the international audience "they deserved", but the process was far from plain sailing. For a start, no one at Disney knew what was in store when *Princess Mononoke* was finished. Violent, morally complex and steeped in Japanese folklore, it was a far cry from *My Neighbour Totoro* and *Kiki's Delivery Service*, the sort of family-friendly films that Disney no doubt thought they were buying into.

As a result, the film would be released in the US by Disney's more edgy, arthouse-leaning subsidiary, Miramax, with localization and distribution overseen by the then infamous, now disgraced, mogul Harvey Weinstein, who reportedly wanted to cut the film from 135 minutes to 90 minutes. It was part of the landmark deal with Disney that Ghibli could veto

any suggested changes to the original films, and Suzuki was no doubt emboldened by that fact when he presented Miramax executives with a special gift: a very realistic-looking replica of a samurai sword. "When Suzuki presented Harvey with the sword," Alpert writes, "Suzuki shouted in English and in a loud voice, '*Mononoke-hime*, NO CUT!'"

Even so, Alpert describes the process of preparing *Princess Mononoke* for international release, and the Tokuma-Disney distribution deal as a whole, as a clash of cultures. Disney's marketing team was reportedly horrified by aspects of Ghibli's films that were relatively innocuous to Japanese audiences, such as a scene in *My Neighbour Totoro* in which the father character bathes with his daughters.

**Above:** The acquisition of *Princess Mononoke* by Disney in the 1990s technically makes San a very unlikely, but undeniable, Disney princess.

THE BLOCKBUSTER SUCCESS OF PRINCESS MONONOKE PROMOTED DIRECTOR HAYAO MIYAZAKI TO A NEW LEVEL OF RENOWN AS BOTH A FILMMAKER AND A PUBLIC FIGURE.

FOR ALL *PRINCESS MONONOKE'S* EPIC SCALE AND COMPLEX THEMES, WHAT WOULD A MIYAZAKI FILM BE WITHOUT A POTENTIALLY CREEPY, MERCHANDISABLE CREATURE? THE DISTINCTIVE KODAMA PERFECTLY FIT THE BILL.

Of the Ghibli canon, *Kiki's Delivery Service* was deemed the least risky proposition, and was prepared for a VHS release, but Alpert himself had to intervene when it became clear that Disney had added extra dialogue, music and sound effects in the process of what should have been a straightforward translation.

Similar changes were suggested, or simply implemented behind Ghibli's back, during the production of the English-language version of *Princess Mononoke*. An initial script draft by author Neil Gaiman was respectful to the spirit of Miyazaki's complex storytelling, but in Alpert's words, "a battle over the script was being waged". Miramax requested

**Above:** With Princess Mononoke's international release came a star-studded English language version. Gillian Anderson, star of *The X-Files* at the time, voiced Moro the wolf god.

changes, adding explanatory plot points and clarifying character motivations and alignments in ways that Miyazaki had kept intentionally ambiguous or opaque. A nine-page list of additional sound effects appeared, covering everything from heavy footsteps and crackling fires to the sound of a cloud passing. The dubbing of *Princess Mononoke* was by accounts tortuous, but ultimately Alpert succeeded in making sure the film was released in a form that was uncut and, largely, unchanged.

*Mononoke's* eventual theatrical release in the US was a drop in the ocean compared to its blockbuster success back home, but the ordeal had been worth it. Suzuki's goal had been achieved, and Studio Ghibli's films were now playing on an international stage, whether the reluctant genius behind their biggest hits wanted them to or not. *Princess Mononoke* premiered at the Berlin and Toronto film festivals, putting in place a new international roll-out strategy that put Ghibli and Miyazaki on a par with other world cinema auteurs. Steve Alpert recalls that, after a screening at the New York Film Festival, Martin Scorsese was keen to meet Miyazaki to discuss filmmaking, and invited him to a post-festival party. Much to his colleagues' disappointment, Miyazaki respectfully declined.

To many commentators, *Princess Mononoke* represents the culmination of a certain phase of Miyazaki's career, but his old colleague and mentor Isao Takahata saw it differently: "He has been reborn." After *Mononoke*, Miyazaki was a record-breaker and an outspoken cultural commentator in his home country, and an ascendant icon of world cinema abroad. How possibly could he, and his Studio, live up to those expectations?

Ghibli had never been as big as *Princess Mononoke*. On a financial, cultural and international scale it made them bigger names than ever before, and creatively the size of their ambition and imagination had never been as large either. It is an enormous film that asks to be wrestled with, there is no binary morality to it, no clear heroes or villains. It doesn't simplify the ungainly nature of violence into a game, or turn spirituality into a magic trick, instead tangling the roots between humanity and its environment into an irreversible knot. In a way, this epic fantasy of gods and monsters from centuries past, is one of Ghibli's truest reflections of the modern world.

Audiences preparing for another charming, light-hearted kids adventure from Miyazaki get a nasty shock at the very start of *Princess Mononoke*. The film begins by hurtling through a forest, tracing a giant feral boar-god with possessed red eyes, and skin that is spewing oily leeches of black ooze. Ashitaka, a young warrior, takes on the boar in a graphic showdown, but in his victory he too becomes infected, his arm injected with a venom of violence. Soon after, Ashitaka's newly superpowered arm fires fierce arrows at oncoming soldiers, who are bloodily dismembered and beheaded, such is the force from his bow. We are not in Totoro's camphor tree anymore. Ashitaka ceremoniously leaves his village and begins a quest to find the mythical Spirit of the Forest, a god of life and death, who he hopes will be able to heal him, but ahead lies a warring

maelstrom of complex and aggressive factions, which he will find himself at the centre of.

In Irontown, a Viking-style stronghold, Ashitaka meets the self-assured but short-sighted Lady Eboshi. She teeters towards the villain end of the character spectrum, but with all of Miyazaki's most interesting creations, her actions make her hard to consolidate. The fact she is a warmonger, one whose bullets directly led to Ashitaka's infection, should make things clear, but her town – which she passionately protects – is progressive and empathetic, providing you're on her side of the fence. Women are given more agency, power and wit than most fantasy outings might offer. The trauma-inducing results of warfare are understood and empathized with. People with leperosy are taken care of here, and later become fiery, bandaged warriors. Irontown has elements of a liberated utopia but at its foundation, as a mining town with monopolistic goals, is a consuming pursuit of power and a militarism that is poisoning the natural world surrounding it.

In that natural world is San, the princess of the wolf-gods, who sees the damage that Irontown is doing to her environment

**Above:** The violent and bloody scenes throughout *Princess Mononoke* made it a very unlikely Disney release. It's no surprise they shifted distribution to their more arthouse, adult-oriented label, Miramax.

**Opposite:** Ashitaka takes aim whilst riding Yakul, his loveable and loyal red elk.

and vehemently protects it. Perhaps more in the hero corner of *Princess Mononoke*'s distorted wrestling ring, she has been raised by wolves, and her feral, animalistic protection of the forest is certainly admirable, but in her rage she takes innocent lives as well, muddying her heroic status. Further complicating this royal rumble are an army of boars seeking vengeance for their fallen god, San's wolf family, a tribe of apes, samurai from a local lord and the fulcrum character of the bloodshed, the Spirit of the Forest. Initially perplexing, the overlaps between rivals and allies highlight the nonsensical value of the human's own conflict in the face of something far greater than themselves. The most impressive sequences of the film are not gifted to war and its futility, but to nature and its far grander, significant power.

In its more earthly form, the Spirit of the Forest has the shape of a deer, with a robin red chest and an uncanny human face. Once the sun sets however, it becomes the Nightwalker, a gigantic, beautiful, iridescent creature that seems to be made of syrup and stars. Within these two forms we witness the enlightening beauty of a creature made of human, natural and supernatural features, and tragically it is one that cannot continue to share a world with the virulence of humanity. The Spirit becomes the focus for the finale, the warriors of the forest aim to protect it, while Eboshi plans to behead it – and she is successful. Shot through the neck, leaving a black hole of a

bullet wound, the Spirit expands high above the treetops like a headless Godzilla and spews more of that unnatural, oily poison across the landscape, destroying forests and towns alike. Ashitaka and San successfully reunite the Spirit with its head, but the damage is done. In a final gift to humanity, the wasteland is converted into blooming greenery, but the Spirit of the Forest and all of the natural gods are dead. The ending may be presented as hopeful, but in the scorched earth that the new blossom sits on is a warning, that the responsibility of care for the earth sits solely with humanity now.

*Princess Mononoke* propelled Ghibli to new creative and financial success, but like the forest, its roots are deep and entwined in history. The women of Irontown, with their chippy determination and glib humour, feel like the adult versions of the forthright kidnapped girls from *Porco Rosso*. The care and emotional resonance towards food shown throughout his films reaches a new level of intimacy, when San maternally chews food for an injured Ashitaka to help feed him. Beyond small character details, the epic fantasy scale of *Nausicaä* and *Laputa: Castle in the Sky* transforms into something weightier here, and the environmental harmony and animist message of *My Neighbour Totoro* is more richly studied. It might be bigger and bolder than the Miyazaki works that came before, but that doesn't mean that *Princess Mononoke* feels like an outsider, it's the perfect evolution.

# MY NEIGHBOURS THE YAMADAS (HŌHOKEKYO TONARI NO YAMADA-KUN, 1999)

## QUE SERA, SERA

DIRECTED BY: ISAO TAKAHATA
WRITTEN BY: ISAO TAKAHATA
LENGTH: 1HR 44MIN
RELEASE DATE (JAPAN): 17 JULY 1999

WHILE ISAO TAKAHATA HAS BEEN DESCRIBED BY HAYAO MIYAZAKI AS HAVING "DESCENDED FROM A GIANT SLOTH", HIS RECORD OF DIRECTING THREE FEATURES FOR GHIBLI IN SIX YEARS – *GRAVE OF THE FIREFLIES, ONLY YESTERDAY* AND *POM POKO* – WAS HARDLY THE WORK OF A SLOUCH. POST-*POM POKO*, THOUGH, YOU CAN SEE HOW HE MIGHT HAVE GARNERED THAT REPUTATION. IT WOULD TAKE FIVE YEARS UNTIL HIS NEXT FILM, *MY NEIGHBOURS THE YAMADAS*, HIT CINEMA SCREENS, THE FIRST OF ONLY TWO FURTHER FILMS HE MADE AT GHIBLI BETWEEN 1994 AND HIS DEATH IN 2018.

By 1999, the blockbusting, record-breaking success of *Princess Mononoke* had irrevocably changed expectations for Studio Ghibli. They'd had hits in the past, but for the first time the industry was expecting another smash. That would come later, of course, with Hayao Miyazaki's *Spirited Away*, but Takahata was left with the thankless task of following a hit as unprecedented as *Mononoke*. Not that *My Neighbours the Yamadas* feels at all affected by the burden of expectation, though. Quietly radical, this adaptation of the long-running newspaper comic strip *Nono-chan* would not just experiment with storytelling structure, weaving short anecdotal skits and sketches into a poetic tapestry of family life, but with animation itself.

Inspired by the Canadian animator Frédéric Back, Takahata wanted to forego the increasingly detailed backgrounds seen in films like Miyazaki's *Princess Mononoke*, in favour of minimal, watercolour-styel backdrops and a negative-space approach that foregrounded the movement of the characters. In his words, "The space will be created by the characters' movement." Likewise, in what would become the defining creative impulse of the filmmaker's final works, Takahata stripped away the polish associated with mainstream animation, looking to reveal the energy and vibrancy of the animators' rough pencil sketches that would usually be erased from the finished work. Ironically, to achieve these most organic of effects, a convoluted and rigorous hybrid production process had to be implemented: hand-drawn linework would be scanned into a computer to be coloured and animated digitally. What resulted was an arduous, labour-intensive and expensive process – and what is commonly referred to as Ghibli's first computer-animated film.

**Opposite:** It might look a bit different to other Ghibli films, but there's lots to embrace in *My Neighbours the Yamadas*.

**Below:** Not a cell phone in sight. Just people living in the moment.

It was also Ghibli's first box-office flop. Sources say that *My Neighbours the Yamadas* cost somewhere in the region of 2 billion yen to make; on release in July 1999, it made merely 1.5 billion yen. Producer Toshio Suzuki blames a switch in distributor from Toho to the "structurally weak" Shochiku, a result of some corporate sabre-rattling on the part of Yasuyoshi Tokuma, head of Ghibli's parent company, Tokuma Shoten, leaving *Yamadas* with a much smaller portfolio of cinema screens nationwide.

However, it's clear from the pre-release materials that Ghibli knew they didn't have another *Mononoke*-sized success on their hands. Doubling down on the inevitable associations with Hayao Miyazaki and his latest hit, a defensive promotional documentary cast *Yamadas* as the perfect complement to *Princess Mononoke*: where Miyazaki's epic adventure was "serious" and didactic, this would be a welcome tonic, described by Takahata in his director's notes as "not a therapy,

but comfort". Even the films' taglines underscored this contrast: *Mononoke*'s "Live" suggests something lofty, whereas the *Yamadas*' "Que Sera, Sera", referencing the Doris Day tune that is sung by characters in the film, is much more easy-going and wholesome.

But far more notable than these comparisons is that *My Neighbours the Yamadas* draws up the dramatis personae for this second half of the Studio Ghibli story, casting Miyazaki as a commercial and pop-cultural powerhouse and Takahata as, essentially, a carte blanche experimental artist, bankrolled by others, and allowed to work at his own sloth-like speed.

**Above:** These slice-of-life vignettes may seem throwaway, but the film's themes run deep.

**Opposite:** The Japanese-language poster for *My Neighbours the Yamadas*.

LIKE THE WARBLER ON THE POSTER FOR *MY NEIGHBOURS THE YAMADAS*, COMPOSER AND POP MUSICIAN AKIKO YANO IS A SONGBIRD WHOSE VOICE AND MUSIC CAN BE HEARD FAR AND WIDE THROUGHOUT THE WORLD OF GHIBLI. AS WELL AS SCORING *YAMADAS* FOR TAKAHATA, YANO GAVE VOICE TO *PONYO*'S TINY SISTERS THAT HELP HER ESCAPE IN THE OPENING ACT OF MIYAZAKI'S MAGICAL ADVENTURE. SHE ALSO PROVIDED HUMAN SOUND EFFECTS FOR TWO SHORT FILMS MADE FOR THE GHIBLI MUSEUM BY HAYAO MIYAZAKI: *HOUSE-HUNTING* AND *MONMON THE WATER SPIDER*.

*My Neighbours the Yamadas* is one of Ghibli's most stunning and most frustrating films. It has moments of unique creativity that are showcases for the craft of animation as a whole, but despite their quality, those moments don't balance out the film's flaws in rhythm and story. That being said, it is unmistakably an Isao Takahata film, and it is one that should be cherished.

Even though it was built in a computer, the first frames of *My Neighbours the Yamadas* are there to make you aware you're watching an animation – there are even little pencils. These pencils draw the sun and then the moon, and from the moon, new lines appear in the shape of Shige, the grandmother of the Yamada family. As the outline moves, colours start being filled in, a line extends from her arm, becoming a dog on a leash, then suddenly, but organically, a street, plants and a neighbour appear in front of her. At the top of the film, we are willed to pay attention to the craft as much as the characters, and in retrospect, viewed as a whole, that balance of focus needed a bit more attention.

This is Takahata in animation sandbox mode, which is exhilarating and exhausting. Takahata is not an animator himself, and as he got older he felt less limited by the constraints of the edges of a page, only by the limits of a concept. Within all the excitement of what could be created, the characters in *My Neighbours the Yamadas* never feel fully realized and the focus seems to be on style, on the grabbing and discarding of ideas, in a breakneck joyride of creative momentum.

The opening minutes are a total joy, in which a wedding speech about the nature of family frames a wildly ambitious, expressive and somehow totally fluid race through life. Mr and Mrs Yamada begin by bob-sleighing through the tiers of their wedding cake, then they transform into sailors on choppy seas, emulating Hokusai's famous *The Great Wave*. On dry land they become farmers, a peach reveals a baby and the chopped branch of a bamboo tree reveals another (an image Takahata would revisit in *The Tale of the Princess Kaguya*). Then, after briefly surfing clouds, being chased by a giant snail, navigating a submarine and some pirates, the Yamada family arrives home. It is breathless in its movement and stupefying in its fluidity. Despite all of the chaos around a family when it's growing, when things are running smoothly on the inside, you barely notice the transitions. Takahata places the simplicity of a family home on the same plane as grand adventures and classical art, that the beauty of domesticity is almost biblical.

The film never recovers from this heady overture. It is full of pluckable moments and ideas, but none as rich in style or theme as here, where form and content coalesce in such a satisfying manner. There are flourishes that join together different chapters of the Yamadas' story, which range

**Above:** Mr Yamada cuts bamboo, playing on the beloved Japanese classic *The Tale of the Bamboo Cutter*, a story that director Isao Takahata would revisit in his final film *The Tale of the Princess Kaguya*.

**Opposite:** Say cheese! Isao Takahata's light hearted portrait of a family captures the magic in the mundane.

from simple devices like narration or title cards to poetry from Matsuo Bashō or Santōka Taneda, and even a hog bounding across from one scene into the next. They are enjoyable in themselves, but the film never sets a template for when one such device will be used. In fact it is unclear when one of the contained stories is actually finished, and combined with extremely varied lengths of the chapters, it makes for a jarring rhythm overall.

It might occasionally be testing as a viewer – particularly some of the more derogatory chapters – but there are moments of inspiration where the film is testing itself, and testing how far audiences will go with it. One sequence involving Mr Yamada's plans to fight some bikers totally shifts the style of the film, from soft graphite, cartoonish and curvy lines with watercolour shading, to harder, scratchier more life-like forms; as if Mr Yamada has gone through his own reverse version of the video for 'Take On Me'.

The film ends with another surreal, cartoonish montage, with the family flying into the clouds while holding umbrellas, before dropping back to reality. Perhaps that's a nice reflection of the film; in moments it will make you fly, then you'll crash back down again for a while. It would be a long time before Takahata's next film *The Tale of the Princess Kaguya*, but from the digital hand-drawn look, to the changing expressionist lines, to the bamboo cutter, and even to the celestial ending, its origins were in the sandbox of *Yamadas*.

# SPIRITED AWAY
## (SEN TO CHIHIRO
## NO KAMIKAKUSHI, 2001)

### A ROAD TO SOMEWHERE

DIRECTED BY HAYAO MIYAZAKI
WRITTEN BY HAYAO MIYAZAKI
LENGTH: 2HR 4MIN
RELEASE DATE (JAPAN): 20 JULY 2001

EVERY FAN REMEMBERS THEIR INTRODUCTION TO THE WORLD OF STUDIO GHIBLI, AND IF YOU'RE READING THIS BOOK, IT'S VERY LIKELY THAT THE FILM THAT FIRST ENRAPTURED AND ENCHANTED YOU WAS *SPIRITED AWAY*. A RECORD-BREAKING SENSATION IN JAPAN – ECLIPSING EVEN THAT OF ITS PREDECESSOR, *PRINCESS MONONOKE* – *SPIRITED AWAY* WAS ALSO THE FIRST GHIBLI FILM TO TRULY BENEFIT FROM A FULL INTERNATIONAL RELEASE, GARNERING THE RESPECT, ACCLAIM AND ACCOLADES THAT, FRANKLY, THE WORK OF HAYAO MIYAZAKI SHOULD HAVE BEEN GETTING ALL ALONG.

**Above:** Packed with delightful detail and extraordinary characters, Studio Ghibli's films are always a feast for the eyes.
**Opposite:** Two tickets please. One child, one otherworldly spirit.

Unsurprisingly, after the intense experience of producing *Princess Mononoke*, Hayao Miyazaki announced his retirement from making feature films in January 1998, but he was far from idle. In 1998 alone, he filmed a travelogue recreating a flight across the Sahara taken by French author and aviator Antoine de Saint-Exupéry; he created his own office space retreat, often referred to as his "atelier", a short walk from the main Studio Ghibli headquarters; he taught a workshop course for aspiring young animation directors age 18–26, called the Higashi Koganei Sonjuku II (following in the footsteps of Isao Takahata, who led a similar course three years prior); and he even started dreaming up plans of a Ghibli Museum dedicated to the craft of animation.

He also, before long, returned to feature filmmaking. Miyazaki was inspired by a holiday with family friends and their young daughters – and the thoroughly unimpressive manga they were reading – to make a film with the modern,

ten-year-old girl in mind. A decade on from *Kiki's Delivery Service*, Miyazaki would return to similar encouraging themes, writing in his November 1999 project proposal:

"This is supposed to be the story of a young girl who is thrown into another world, where good and bad people are co-existing. In this world, she undergoes rigorous training, learns about friendship and self-sacrifice, and using her own basic smarts, somehow not only survives but manages to return to our world..."

However, the world had changed since 1989, and Miyazaki's social conscience and conflicted worldview would be reflected in the work. "Our world appears ever more fuzzy and confusing," he wrote.

Left: A rainy scene in Jiufen, Taiwan, with architecture similar to that of the locales in *Spirited Away*. After the success of the film, local business and tourist boards played up the similarity, although Hayao Miyazaki himself reportedly denies any connection between the film and the town.

Below: Just when you thought it was safe to go back in the water: Chihiro gets swept away.

Opposite: The Japanese-language poster for *Spirited Away*.

"Yet in spite of that it threatens to corrode and devour us. The job of this film is, therefore, to depict this world with clarity within a fantasy framework."

Inspiration for the design of *Spirited Away*'s eerie spirit world would come from the Edo-Tokyo Open Air Architectural Museum in Tokyo's Koganei Park, just a short drive from Studio Ghibli's offices, "I feel nostalgic here," Miyazaki would say. "Especially when I stand here alone in the evening, near closing time, and the sun is setting – tears well up in my eyes."

By Miyazaki's standards, production progressed slowly, not helped by the endless stream of ideas and characters that poured out of the director's imagination. He would later describe the storyboarding process as if "a lid on my brain – one that I normally never open – has been opened, and that an electrical current connects me to some other faraway place."

At one point, even with elements of animation outsourced to multiple studios in Japan and Korea, it looked unlikely that

**Previous pages:** Now that's what we call a double-page spread.

**Opposite:** Shoes off on the carpet. Chihiro charges through Yubaba's lair.

the film would hit its projected release date in July 2001. The director and a few senior members of the crew held an impromptu story conference in which Miyazaki laid out the sprawling, detailed, developing story. As usual, animation had started before Miyazaki had fully finished his script and storyboards, and it was only once he talked the team through the rest of the plot that it hit him. "Oh no," Toshio Suzuki recalls Miyazaki exclaiming, "this is a three-hour movie."

Suzuki, now a seasoned producer and master manipulator, suggested that they could postpone the release, knowing that such a suggestion would spur Miyazaki on. And it worked. Instead, they would throw out the back half of the story and refocus. Reviewing the animation that had already been completed, Miyazaki was attracted to a background character, a "weird-looking masked man" who is seen floating across the bathhouse bridge near the start of the film. Years later, Suzuki could still recall the date. "It was May 3, 2000. That's the day that No-Face became a central character."

Thanks to this shift in direction and renewed focus, *Spirited Away* hit its July 2001 release date. At a press conference marking the premiere of the film, Miyazaki would start the proceedings in a playful mood, saying, "Well, here I am again, someone who only four years ago announced that he would be retiring." He had good reason to feel upbeat: *Spirited Away* was an instant hit, grossing over 30 billion yen in 2001, about as much as the next five top-grossers, including *A.I. Artificial Intelligence*, *Pearl Harbor*, *Hannibal* and *Planet of the Apes*, added together.

In Japan, *Spirited Away's* takings surpassed those of both *Princess Mononoke* and James Cameron's *Titanic*, the two blockbusters that in 1997 battled for supremacy atop the table of the most successful films in Japanese box office history. For almost twenty years, *Spirited Away* remained the highest-grossing film of all time in Japan, with its record first challenged by Makoto Shinkai's *Your Name* in 2016, and then broken by the manga spin-off *Demon Slayer: Kimetsu no Yaiba the Movie: Mugen Train*, which gathered unstoppable box office momentum in 2020.

*Spirited Away's* success in Japan was historic, but while its international release might have brought in less money, it was no less groundbreaking. It was the first animated film to compete at the Berlin Film Festival, where it won the prestigious top prize, the Golden Bear. Miyazaki was reluctant to travel, and even less reluctant to attend awards ceremonies, so it fell to Ghibli's resident foreigner, Steve Alpert, to accept many of the thirty-six awards the film received.

Alpert writes a very entertaining account of his time at the centre of the whirlwind of *Spirited Away's* international acclaim in his memoir *Sharing a House with the Never-Ending Man*, acting as an unlikely stand-in for the absent genius ("some of you may have noticed, I'm not Japanese", he said, accepting the Golden Bear), and then trying, and ultimately failing, to coax Miyazaki into attending perhaps the most important of all ceremonies: the Academy Awards.

Even without the director in attendance, the film took home the Oscar for Best Animated Feature, to date the only non-English-language film to do so. Miyazaki later issued a statement that implicitly commented on the US's involvement in the 2003 invasion of Iraq:

"The world currently faces a very unfortunate situation, and I am therefore sorry that I cannot experience the full joy of receiving this award. However, I am deeply grateful to all my friends for the efforts they have made so that *Spirited Away* could be shown in America, and also to all those who rated my film so highly."

Following the deal between Disney and Studio Ghibli's parent company, Tokuma Shoten, and the steep learning curve that was the Miramax release of *Princess Mononoke*, by all accounts the international rollout of *Spirited Away* progressed

much more smoothly. For one, Ghibli had a strong advocate in the form of Pixar chief and long-term Miyazaki admirer John Lasseter, who executive produced an English-language dub directed by Disney veteran Kirk Wise (*Beauty and the Beast*, *The Hunchback of Notre Dame*).

Even with this support in place, Disney didn't quite know how to effectively market and release the film, landing somewhere between family-friendly adventure and esteemed arthouse gem, lacking the promotional heft of their own animated classics. A limited release in late 2002 was followed by a wider 700-screen re-release to capitalize on the Oscar win,

yet despite strong notices from influential critics such as Roger Ebert, the film grossed just $10 million – under five per cent of its Japanese total.

In the end, *Spirited Away* wasn't destined to become an international blockbuster, but the catbus was out of the bag. A box office behemoth back home, and a widely revered award winner abroad, the film succeeded in introducing a new, global audience to Studio Ghibli as it came to cinemas, television screens and DVD players across the West. For many, it was their first and strongest hit of Miyazaki magic, and they never looked back.

*Spirited Away* contains two giant-headed identical twin witches, a boiler room operator with six arms, a boy who can turn into a dragon, and a gargantuan buffet-inhaling monster. But its most magical moment comes when a young girl, having navigated her way through this world of spirits, rests her eyes on a beautiful, darkened horizon and softly, satisfyingly, bites into a red bean cake. Suddenly, in this moment all of the fantasy that came before feels less so, and starts to feel more real, because it shares a world with this simple human moment. That is what Studio Ghibli is so remarkable at: they place the fantastically imaginative alongside earthly realism and in doing so make the sublime attainable and the mundane magical. *Spirited Away* is Ghibli's unique ability to enchant at its most concentrated and it can be overwhelming even, but as an intense blast of their powerful creativity, it is unparalleled.

The film begins in familiar, tried and tested Ghibli territory, with a family in their car moving to a new home. If the magical journey of *My Neighbour Totoro* started like that, why risk changing the formula? In the backseat is the prickly ten-year-old Chihiro, who has little in the way of adventurous spirit and whose strident personality is at odds with Ghibli's typical protagonists. A diversion leads the family to step into an abandoned theme park, a location that provided a beacon of exploitative consumerism to skewer in Isao Takahata's *Pom Poko* seven years prior, now left to crumble in a precursor to the film's relationship with excess. Here, Chihiro's parents

take a seat in a restaurant that's empty of customers, but full of food, and furiously help themselves. What follows is one of Miyazaki's most upsetting moments, that recalls the end of *Animal Farm*, as in their sloppy, inhaling greed the two humans turn into pigs. When discovered by Chihiro their faces have swelled to fill the frame. Horrified by the sight, a young boy called Haku tells her to find refuge by taking up work in the nearby bathhouse.

It is in this bathhouse that Chihiro's liminal journey truly begins. Her first encounter is with Kamaji, the multi-limbed man who keeps the bathhouse boiler going with the help of some cameo-making soot sprites. Kamaji's abode is dirty, haphazard and hidden away in the basement, its rusty appearance kept in the shadow of the regal bathhouse. Despite being essential to its continued operation, the ugly production line is never encountered in the facade of the attendees – perhaps Kamaji is a vessel for Ghibli's animators?

Safely inside, Chihiro heads to the witch (and site manager) Yubaba, to negotiate herself a job. The opposite of Kamaji, Yubaba sits at the top of the house, in a lavish room overspilling with trinkets, her grandiose outfit and jewellery matching her extravagant interior design taste. Yubaba is the trickier side of two magical siblings, the calmer Zeniba completing the pair, making the duo reminiscent of the Wicked Witches of the East and West from *The Wizard of Oz*. Yubaba is another Ghibli character who is non-compliant when trying to squeeze into

a villainous box. She is ostentatious and vindictive, but her treatment of her children and her customers shows genuine care, and she even shows a sliver of pride in Chihiro too. Like all good antagonists, with her comical cackle, spiky dialogue and cartoonishly colossal head, she is desperately entertaining. And she sets Chihiro to work.

Being fresh on the job doesn't help Chihiro. She's thrown in at the deep end with a stink spirit, a hefty lump of mobile sludge who has arrived for a scrub, and whose stench has made the other staff scarper and any nearby food rotten. In an act of heroic grace, like plucking a thorn from the paw of a bear, Chihiro dives into the spirit's bath and finds the handlebars of a bicycle awkwardly stabbing its side and pulls them out. This releases a beautifully animated, swelling tidal wave of muddy ooze and human junk, revealing that the being was in fact a river spirit that had merely become polluted. This act slightly ingratiates Chihiro to the bathhouse, and combines the films dual themes of consumerism and environmentalism, the excessive garbage and expendable attitude of humanity, poisoning nature until it is unrecognizable.

**Above:** The bathhouse from *Spirited Away* is a strong contender for Ghibli's most memorable location, seen here as an imposing scale model at a temporary exhibition about architecture in Studio Ghibli's movies at the Edo-Tokyo Open-Air Architectural Museum.

**Opposite:** No-Face, one of Ghibli's most iconic characters, stands on the bathhouse bridge.

Similarly effective, although more so in its gorging than its purging, is No-Face. An iconic Ghibli creation, after being secretly welcomed into the bathhouse by Chihiro, this simple black figure consumes all food within sight. It rapidly balloons into an insatiable goth Jabba the Hutt, flinging gold at the same rate it gobbles entire buffet tables and the occasional staff member. The workers initially remain blind to the damage the spirit is actually doing, happily dancing in the downpour of gold. Creations like the stink spirit and No-Face fill the bathhouse with thrilling excess – and following in the mop marks of *My Neighbour Totoro* the cleaning that goes alongside makes for an extremely satisfying watch too. After work, Chihiro enjoys her quiet, red bean reward. It's one of a few moments where the film relaxes, a necessary breath between shifts. A later train ride across a mirrored, amber sea is an ethereal, meditative inhale of calm, and a rice ball shared between friends is as much a remedy for the soul as any medicine.

Although the moments of dramatic reprieve do help, *Spirited Away* remains an incredibly busy film, and the price to pay for the exemplary character design and imaginative animation is a convoluted and slightly unrewarding plot. The overflowing bathhouse, its residents and their individual stories and allegiances become lost in the feast of creativity, and when a rushed loose-end-tying finale is attempted outside the doors of the bathhouse, its execution is anything but clean. But it's not in narrative cohesion that the joys of *Spirited Away* are to be found. It is set in a bathhouse and is best experienced by letting it wash over you.

# THE CAT RETURNS
# (NEKO NO ONGAESHI, 2002)

## FELINE FAIRY-TALE FARE

DIRECTED BY HIROYUKI MORITA
WRITTEN BY REIKO YOSHIDA
LENGTH: 1HR 15MIN
RELEASE DATE (JAPAN): 19 JULY 2002

RELEASED IN JAPANESE CINEMAS A YEAR TO THE DAY AFTER *SPIRITED AWAY'S* BLOCKBUSTER OPENING, *THE CAT RETURNS* IS AN ODD ENTRY IN THE STUDIO GHIBLI CANON, WITH A UNIQUE BACKSTORY.

Reportedly, Studio Ghibli had been approached by a theme park in 1999 with a request for a 20-minute animated short centred around a single theme: cats. "The Cat Project" would develop into a pseudo-sequel to 1995's *Whisper of the Heart*, when Hayao Miyazaki himself suggested that key characters and locations would be lifted from Yoshifumi Kondō's teen romance, chiefly the dashing Baron.

Aoi Hiiragi, the author of the manga that *Whisper of the Heart* was adapted from, was brought on board to create a follow-up work. The resulting manga was not a straightforward sequel, more a sort of story that could have been dreamed up by Shizuku, the young girl with a hyper-active imagination from *Whisper of the Heart*.

The theme park tie-in fizzled out, but the Cat Project purred on, retooled as a potential showcase for up-and-coming talent at the Studio. Hiiragi's manga, published by Ghibli's parent company Tokuma Shoten, was much longer than anticipated, so it was mooted that the film could instead be a 45-minute straight-to-video short.

Veteran animator and long-time freelancer Hiroyuki Morita – whose previous Studio Ghibli work included in-between animation on *Kiki's Delivery Service* and key animation for *My Neighbours the Yamadas*, as well as credits on non-Ghibli classics ranging from *Akira* to *Perfect Blue* – was chosen to direct. It was Morita's extensive storyboards and ambitious planning proposal that convinced producer Toshio Suzuki to bump up the short to a feature-length runtime, and prep it for a full-scale cinema release, confident that the resulting film would be a hit.

Suzuki's confidence was well-founded. While it couldn't possibly match *Spirited Away's* record-breaking takings, *The Cat Returns* grossed a respectable 6.4 billion yen in 2002, making it by far the best-performing Japanese film at the domestic box office that year. In the final tallies, it was bested only by gigantic Hollywood blockbusters, including *Harry Potter and the Chamber of Secrets*, *Spider-Man* and *The Lord of the Rings: The Two Towers*. In comparison, Ghibli's slight, 75-minute feature – presented as a double bill with the second episode of the "Ghiblies" series of comic sketches about Studio life, in order to fill out the theatrical programme – must have seemed refreshingly modest.

Despite the success of his debut film, Hiroyuki Morita returned to life as a freelancer, later coming back to Ghibli to work on Takahata's *The Tale of the Princess Kaguya*. At time of writing, he has yet to direct another feature. *The Cat Returns*, however, received an international push bolstered by *Spirited Away's* Oscar-winning success, featuring a star-studded dub with Anne Hathaway, Tim Curry, and Cary Elwes as the Baron himself. For many younger viewers in the West, it was one of their first exposures to Studio Ghibli, and, as its DVD came to certain markets before *Whisper of the Heart*, its pseudo-sequel status became, for a time, something of a footnote.

**Opposite:** Cat-Man Returns for Ghibli's first sequel.

**Below:** Throughout their entire filmography, Ghibli have created a veritable buffet of classic food moments. Here, Muta gets a trifle carried away.

In theory, *The Cat Returns* should be an ideal Ghibli film, and it has all the ingredients. A young female protagonist searching for her place in the world, a magical realm that's just beyond our own, a buffet of bright culinary delights and, of course, lots and lots of cats. But perhaps it's because those are the exact ingredients we expect to go into a Ghibli film, and because *The Cat Returns* doesn't inject the recipe with much flare, what we end up with is more of a dull Ghibli ready meal. Ghibli's "failures" like *My Neighbours the Yamadas* or *Tales from Earthsea* are admirable in their creative ambition, even if they falter. Unfortunately, *The Cat Returns* is something rarer even than the Ghibli "failure", it is a Ghibli lacking imagination. The look of *The Cat Returns* is instantly jarring, as if a Miyazaki film has been put through a circus mirror that stretches out your body, the people here are ganglier and the overall style more outwardly cartoonish. The story too seems to be misshapen. Ghibli works like *Spirited Away* or *Whisper of the Heart* take elements of a fish-out-of-water fantasy narrative, as in *Alice in Wonderland*, but adjusts them to modern sensibilities and themes, doing away with the shackles of narrative tradition, diverting into unknown, ambitious, idiosyncratic territory.

*The Cat Returns* is simpler, following Haru, a young girl who saves a cat Prince from being run over and becomes betrothed to him. She travels through magic kingdoms, survives sword fights, dines at royal banquets and navigates a hedge maze in a pleasant stroll through fairy-tale fare. It is a rigid story where being "cool" is a desirable characteristic and combat is a reliable solution to life's problems, the narrative flexibility or moral exploration we have come to expect from the studio remaining absent. Additionally disappointing is the film's use of characters from *Whisper of the Heart*, who here become heightened caricatures of lavish pomp in the case of the Baron, or a bumbling oaf in the case of Muta. Their legacy isn't exactly turned into tatters, but it's certainly left a bit bruised.

The film is certainly not without redeeming features though. The Cat Kingdom can be found just by wandering city streets in the correct way, placing the adventure within tantalizing reach and staying true to Ghibli's approach of blending the magic and the everyday. Within the kingdom itself, the bedraggled and bizarre Cat King reigns with intoxicatedly chaotic and entertaining power, but he is not enough to make up for the seemingly improvised final act. New characters and backstory reveals sustain the film's hand-to-mouth relationship to the plot, before it ends on perhaps its most striking image. Recalling *Kiki's Delivery Service*, Haru – tumbling through the sky – synchronizes with a flock of birds and uses them like an avian spiral staircase to descend safely to earth. It is a beautiful moment, and a nice one to remember the film by, even if it is not one to desperately return to.

**Above:** Baron and Haru on the crow staircase. A stand out moment in a work that doesn't hit Ghibli's regular high flying quality.

**Opposite:** The Japanese-language poster for *The Cat Returns*.

猫の国。それは、自分の時間を
生きられないやつの行くところ。
猫になっても、いいんじゃないッ？

# 猫の恩返し

スタジオジブリ作品
STUDIO GHIBLI

宮崎 駿 企画 ● 森田宏幸 第一回監督作品
池脇千鶴 ● 袴田吉彦 ● 前田亜季／山田孝之／佐藤仁美／岡江久美子 ● 丹波哲郎

原作 柊あおい「バロン 猫の男爵」（徳間書店刊）● 脚本 吉田玲子 ● 音楽 野見祐二 ● 主題歌「風になる」つじあやの（スピードスターレコーズ）● 作画監督 井上鋭 ● 美術監督 田中直哉 ● 特別協賛 ハウス食品 ● 特別協力 ローソン ● 配給 東宝
製作プロデューサー 鈴木敏夫 ● 制作 スタジオジブリ ● 徳間書店・スタジオジブリ・日本テレビ・電通・ブエナビスタ ホームエンターテイメント・三菱商事・東宝 提携作品

# HOWL'S MOVING CASTLE
# (HAURU NO UGOKU SHIRO, 2004)

## THE ULTIMATE MOBILE HOME

DIRECTED BY HAYAO MIYAZAKI
WRITTEN BY HAYAO MIYAZAKI
LENGTH: 1HR 59MIN
RELEASE DATE (JAPAN): 20 NOVEMBER 2004

IN JULY 2001, AT A PRESS CONFERENCE MARKING THE IMMINENT RELEASE OF *SPIRITED AWAY*, HAYAO MIYAZAKI ANNOUNCED HE WAS RETIRING FROM DIRECTING FEATURE-LENGTH FILMS. INSTEAD, HIS EFFORTS WOULD GO TOWARDS THE SOON-TO-OPEN GHIBLI MUSEUM, CURATING SPECIAL EXHIBITIONS AND CREATING SHORT FORM WORK TO SCREEN IN THE MUSEUM'S IN-HOUSE CINEMA. DIRECTING WAS A YOUNG MAN'S GAME, AND IT WAS TIME FOR A NEW GENERATION TO TAKE OVER.

That September, it was announced that Studio Ghibli's next feature project would be *Howl's Moving Castle*, an adaptation of the English-language children's fantasy by Welsh author Diana Wynne Jones. With Miyazaki ostensibly retired, the role of director went to the promising young filmmaker Mamoru Hosoda, who could trace his entire career in animation back to a seed of influence planted by Miyazaki's 1979 feature-length debut, *Lupin III: The Castle of Cagliostro*.

In fact, Hosoda had initially applied to work at Ghibli as an animator, but received a personal rejection from Miyazaki that encouraged him to develop his craft elsewhere, and so

**Above:** A connection is formed between the film's two protagonists: the wizard Howl and Sophie, an unfortunate victim of a malevolent curse.
**Opposite:** From its turrets to its metal chicken feet, the moving castle is another captivating Miyazaki creation.

Hosoda spent the 1990s at Toei Animation, sharpening his skills as an animator on the *Dragon Ball Z* and *Sailor Moon* franchises, before co-directing the popular *Digimon: The Movie* in 2000. Could he be the next Miyazaki?

Not at Ghibli, that's for sure. By the end of 2002, Hosoda was out, Miyazaki was back in, and the whole *Howl's Moving*

ふたりが暮らした。

宮崎 駿 監督作品

ハウルの動く城

HOWL'S
MOVING CASTLE

ソフィー／倍賞千恵子 ● ハウル／木村拓哉 ● 荒地の魔女／美輪明宏

*Castle* project changed course. The timeline reproduced in Ghibli's *The Art of Howl's Moving Castle* book neglects to mention this aborted production, instead airbrushing the history to start with a research trip to Europe in September 2002, followed by Miyazaki's own script, storyboarding and concept sketches from November onwards, with production starting in earnest in February 2003.

Being kicked off *Howl's Moving Castle* was only a temporary setback for Hosoda, who would eventually become one of Japanese animation's most successful, respected and original voices, starting with 2006's *The Girl Who Leapt Through Time*, through *Summer Wars*, *Wolf Children* and *The Boy and the Beast*, to the Oscar-nominated *Mirai*. Looking back, Hosoda sees the experience as a key part of his growth as a filmmaker, and describes it as a classic case of creative differences:

"I was told to make [the movie] similar to how Miyazaki would have made it, but I wanted to make my own film the way I wanted to make it. The difference between the film I wanted to do and how they wanted to do it was too great, so I had to get off the project."

And so, not for the first or last time, Miyazaki's retirement proved to be short-lived and, like with *Kiki's Delivery Service*, it came at the expense of a younger filmmaker's work. When asked about this tendency at the Venice Film Festival premiere of the finished *Howl's Moving Castle*, Miyazaki explained "I've got this nasty part of me that makes me want to do a little bit more."

*Howl's Moving Castle* was released in November 2004 and was a resounding hit at the Japanese box office, and while it didn't match *Spirited Away*'s totals, at time of writing it is still one of the highest-grossing Japanese films of all time. It managed to do this without Toshio Suzuki's usual aggressive advertising campaign – reportedly in response to an outburst from Miyazaki following a suggestion in a staff meeting that *Spirited Away*'s success was, at least partly, down to a smart marketing campaign.

**Opposite:** The Japanese-language poster for *Howl's Moving Castle*.

**Below:** From giant bird and young girl, to trim wizard and wizened housekeeper, Howl and Sophie transform throughout the film.

Miyazaki was clearly in a grave mood, greatly affected by ongoing international conflict. In what should have been a victory-lap interview with the *Guardian*'s Xan Brooks, he described his contemporary worldview in dark terms:

"Personally I am very pessimistic. But when, for instance, one of my staff has a baby you can't help but bless them for a good future. Because I can't tell that child, 'Oh, you shouldn't have come into this life.' And yet I know the world is heading in a bad direction. So with those conflicting thoughts in mind, I think about what kind of films I should be making."

This unresolvable conflict is on full display in *Howl's Moving Castle*, in particular in Miyazaki's adaptation, which veered into darker territory than Wynne Jones' original. Unlike many other authors who have had their work adapted by Ghibli, though, Wynne Jones was diplomatic, even insightful, in how she viewed the film:

"Miyazaki and I were both children in World War II and we seem to have gone opposite ways in our reactions to it. I tend to leave the actual war out, whereas Miyazaki has his cake and eats it, representing both the nastiness of a war and the exciting scenic effects of a big bombing raid."

The next English-language fantasy author whose work Ghibli chose to adapt wouldn't be quite so forgiving.

**Above:** Hayao Miyazaki, holding the Golden Lion for Lifetime Achievement awarded by the Venice Film Festival.

**Left:** Christian Bale (voice of Howl) was already a Ghibli fan, having reportedly loved *Spirited Away*.

**Right:** Howl holds Calcifer, who is in possession of his heart. For many viewers Calcifer is also the heart of the film.

## REVIEW: HOWL'S MOVING CASTLE

How do you successfully follow the first non-English language film to win the Academy Award for Best Animated Feature? You don't. Well, at least not successfully. Perhaps it's the crisis that befalls many a retiree, but *Howl's Moving Castle* feels like Miyazaki returning just to relive the greatest hits of his younger years. In the wake of huge critical and commercial success, rather than expand the horizons of the studio, he just takes them back to their old haunts.

Here's the thing about Ghibli's old haunts though. They're pretty nice. From the pan-European setting, to the gravity defying aircraft and even to the delicious cooked breakfast, *Howl's Moving Castle* cruises through perfect Ghibli home comforts, and it is so easily watchable. But who wants a Hayao Miyazaki film that is just OK?

The film is set during wartime, a war in which the details seem to be fairly hazy, the destruction of combat overshadowing the reasoning. It is perhaps what Miyazaki wanted, to mirror the devastation of war (stoked by the events in Iraq of the time), along with the confusion, obliviousness and capricious egos of the people at the centre of them. However, the war becomes more like background fodder that allows the director to place his beloved airship sketches into combat, even if in relation to the characters they seem inessential.

The ships themselves, which recall Miyazaki's designs from *Nausicaä* and *Castle in the Sky* balance a curious heft and delicacy, featuring iron barrel chests and metal butterfly wings, as if they themselves are torn between the grotesqueries of war and natural beauty. Caught in their looming shadows is Sophie, a young hat maker, who becomes cursed by a witch – the Witch of the Waste – to look much older than she appears. And, in a self-imposed exile, she takes refuge in a strange building that seems to be able to walk.

This is Howl's castle, the titular role, and it is a wonderful creation. A huge patchwork of iron panelling, stone turrets, quaint brick cottage facades, large fabric wings and impossibly tiny metal chicken-like feet. Despite its size, this hulking beast of a palace can instantly transport and transform too, becoming a city storefront or a gateway to a serene grass valley. It is a Miyazaki vision of utopian industry, an idealized habitat brought together through magic, that balances clashing artificial textures and makes them into something living.

Here Sophie meets a new family, a young boy called Markl (who also alters his appeared age, although by choice), a fiery fire spirit called Calcifer who keeps the castle running and the mid-2000s emo idol himself, the stubbornly independent wizard Howl. Howl is fighting in the ongoing war, using a toxic curse that turns him into a large bird that can navigate the flying machines and their bombs. Compared to *Princess Mononoke*'s Ashitaka who wants to negotiate peace, Howl is on the front line, perhaps unintentionally rendered as heroic, an unnecessary martyr for the confusing cause.

It is within the castle walls that the film shines, quite literally in fact, as Sophie cleans it from top to bottom in one memorably satisfying sequence. She manages to tame Calcifer's flames to help cook a sizzling, stomach-growlingly delicious plate of bacon and eggs for the house. Later, when the Witch of the Waste becomes part of the home, now also in great old age, Sophie becomes her carer. It is a relationship of respect and humanity, as the witch's original cursing of Sophie becomes a forgotten footnote, in a touching act of parental support.

In these pursuits to help those around her, rather than just herself, Sophie in turn tames Howl's flaming vanity as well. However, although her autonomy is clear, Sophie does come to be defined by her acts for others. Compared to the forthright adventurers of San, Chihiro and Kiki before her, and despite the great possibilities in Howl's world, Sophie's are limited to the unequal land of the domestic.

Unsurprisingly, considering where Miyazaki was in his life at this point, there is a great respect for elders in the film. Sophie gains more confidence after being cursed, Markl is respected when he dons an old man disguise and the Witch of the Waste turns from hissable villain to charmingly unstable grandmother figure. In *Howl's Moving Castle*, age doesn't mean that you have to become a supporting character, and Miyazaki would take that to heart. He might have gotten old, he might have even retired (and retired again, and again), but some of his future works would firmly re-establish him as the hero.

**Opposite, Above:** The dog Heen, the young boy Markl and Turnip-Head round out Howl's merry band of travellers.

**Opposite, Below:** When Sophie Met Calcifer. The fire demon is voiced by Billy Crystal in the English-language version.

### GHIBLI AND AARDMAN

GHIBLI HAS A FAMOUSLY CLOSE RELATIONSHIP WITH PIXAR, BUT THEY ALSO HAVE A STRONG ADMIRATION FOR AARDMAN ANIMATIONS. GHIBLI HAS RELEASED AARDMAN'S WORK IN JAPAN, AND THE GHIBLI MUSEUM DEDICATED AN EXHIBITION TO WALLACE AND GROMIT IN 2006. IRONICALLY, AT THAT YEAR'S OSCARS, *HOWL'S MOVING CASTLE* WAS NOMINATED FOR BEST ANIMATED FEATURE BUT LOST OUT TO AARDMAN'S *WALLACE AND GROMIT: CURSE OF THE WERE-RABBIT*.

# TALES FROM EARTHSEA (GEDO SENKI, 2006)

## MIYAZAKI VS MIYAZAKI

DIRECTED BY GORŌ MIYAZAKI
WRITTEN BY GORŌ MIYAZAKI & KEIKO NIWA
LENGTH: 1HR 55MIN
RELEASE DATE (JAPAN): 29 JULY 2006

FOLLOWING *HOWL'S MOVING CASTLE*, YOU GUESSED IT, HAYAO MIYAZAKI
ANNOUNCED HIS RETIREMENT. AND AT LEAST FOR ONE PROJECT, HE STUCK TO IT.
CONTINUING IN A VEIN THAT WOULD COME TO DEFINE LATE-PERIOD GHIBLI, THE
STUDIO'S NEXT PROJECT WOULD ALSO ADAPT A NOVEL BY AN ENGLISH-LANGUAGE
AUTHOR WHO ONCE PROVED PIVOTAL AND INFLUENTIAL TO MIYAZAKI.

**Above:** Beautiful but sparse. *Tales From Earthsea* looks amazing
but is lacking when it comes to its story.
**Opposite:** Prince Arren, the son of a great leader, shoulders the
story for Hayao Miyazaki's son Goro's directorial debut.

He'd originally tried, and failed, to secure the rights for an
animated adaptation of Ursula K. Le Guin's *Tales from Earthsea*
series in the early 1980s, and he'd later say that books from the
fantasy series were a consistent presence on his bedside table,
influencing much of his work from *Nausicaä of the Valley of the
Wind* onwards.

It wasn't until the international success of both *My
Neighbour Totoro* and *Spirited Away* that Le Guin warmed
up to the idea of a Miyazaki adaptation of *Earthsea*, and in
August 2005, Miyazaki and Toshio Suzuki visited the author
and obtained her blessing. The catch, though, was that the
director of the film wouldn't be *Hayao* Miyazaki, it would be...
*Gorō* Miyazaki, his son.

Who is Gorō Miyazaki? At this point, he was in his late
thirties, and hadn't followed his father into animation. In fact, this
project would be his first film credit, full stop. By all accounts
he'd always been a doodler and was a disciple of anime and
manga, but he trained as a landscaper, and worked designing
parks and gardens as a construction consultant. His relationship

with Ghibli had started with the Ghibli Museum, for which
Gorō served as project manager and inaugural director from
2001–2005.

The elder Miyazaki believed that he'd used up all of his
ideas for adapting *Earthsea* in his previous films, so thought this
was a good opportunity to test out some new talent. But if this
reads like nepotism, rest assured that Hayao strongly opposed
Gorō's appointment as director of the film. The younger
Miyazaki's strongest support came from producer Toshio
Suzuki, who impressed on his old colleague the importance
of inspiration over experience. "I am aware this appointment
is a reckless one," he recalled in his memoirs. "But he ran the
museum so successfully without experience. So I believe he can
make an interesting film."

Throughout production, Gorō Miyazaki kept an extensive blog, with whole entries dedicated to his relationship with his father. One, titled "Hayao Miyazaki, to me, is 'Zero Marks as a Father, Full Marks as a Director'", painted a bleak family portrait: "My father was almost never at home. My father threw himself completely into his work. That's why, from my earliest awareness to the present day, I hardly ever had the chance to talk to him."

Gorō says he received no advice from his father, and, in fact, they avoided each other throughout the production. At the staff screening of the finished film, Hayao walked out halfway through for a cigarette. While Miyazaki senior did return and watch the rest of the film, he was heard to say afterwards: "I saw my own child. He hasn't become an adult. That's all. It's good that he made one movie. With that, he should stop." Gorō wouldn't receive any personal feedback from his father for three days, until a note came via another Ghibli employee that said that the film "was made in an honest manner... And it was good."

Much has been made of the father–son conflict between the Miyazakis. Helen McCarthy, anime expert and author of *Hayao Miyazaki: Master of Japanese Animation*, once presented the theory that it was all for show: a rumour-mill ground by Toshio Suzuki to sell tickets, much as the promotion of Gorō to director of his own film was, reportedly, inspired by a consumer survey that placed "Miyazaki" high among other household Japanese brand names. Whether we buy into these theories or not, it's clear that Suzuki, recently installed (against

his wishes) as president of a newly independent Ghibli, clearly had his eye on the future prospects of the Studio.

The gambit paid off, but wasn't without cost. Released in July 2006, the film was a hit, ending the year as the highest-grossing Japanese film at the national box office – but it also won the Japanese equivalent of the Golden Raspberry for both Worst Film and Director of the year. At the Japanese Academy Awards, it lost to *The Girl Who Leapt Through Time*, a film from Mamoru Hosoda, the director originally lined up to direct *Howl's Moving Castle* for Ghibli, before Miyazaki gave him the boot.

*Tales from Earthsea* now occupies the unique position in the Ghibli catalogue of being commonly known as "the bad one". Out of all the mixed and negative reviews, perhaps the most scathing comes from Le Guin herself:

"It does not have the delicate accuracy of *Totoro* or the powerful and splendid richness of detail of *Spirited Away*... Much of it was, I thought, incoherent. The filmmakers treated these books as mines for names and a few concepts, taking bits and pieces out of context, and replacing the story/ies with an entirely different plot, lacking in coherence and consistency. I wonder at the disrespect shown not only to the books but to their readers."

**Opposite:** The Japanese-language poster for *Tales from Earthsea*.

**Below:** From landscape architect to an architect of animated fantasy, Goro Miyazaki follows his father into the family trade.

## REVIEW: TALES FROM EARTHSEA

He might give his father full marks as a director, but Gorō Miyazaki hasn't quite earned himself the same high score. Yet in spite of what some may say, his first film *Tales from Earthsea* does at least warrant a passing grade. It absolutely has its flaws, and it does struggle with the weight of its own context from both Ursula K. Le Guin's texts and the Miyazaki name, but it doesn't buckle, and it doesn't deserve its reputation as Ghibli's black sheep. You have to respect Gorō for stepping up to the plate, and even more so when you start watching it and realize one of the first scenes features a son killing his father.

It begins with a quote on screen, an adage of *Earthsea's* world philosophy that mentions the immense value of light, and the film takes this message from on high and injects it through its skies, waves and streets. Swathes, beams and speckles of light pour through the film in deft and evangelical ways. Were it a silent film one might be misguided into thinking Le Guin's text was being treated with the regality it deserved. The unrolling of *Earthsea* before our eyes is magical. An aged coastal town, littered with the tumbling shadows of old tin mines feels like a Cornish postcard. Golden sheets of enormous sand dunes are curiously dotted with the timber corpses of a forgotten naval fleet. The urban hub of Hort Town feels like a hybrid of city planning between Istanbul, Venice and the Gardens of Babylon, the overlapping sprawl of brick matched by lush greenery blooming through it. The locations aren't gleaming, they're elegance having degraded through time, resulting in a real sense of history emanating from each new setting.

As one glorious vista unfurls the next, the scale of the world feels enormous, until one small issue causes it all to collapse: telling a story. Despite its size, Earthsea seems to

be only populated by a handful of people, who apparently live right next to each other. If the Shire backed on to Mordor in *The Lord of the Rings*, Frodo's journey wouldn't seem so spectacular would it?

There is a central battle going on between a young prince, a young girl, an old wizard, another old wizard and a quest for eternal life, but despite how much they talk about it, it's not entirely clear what is happening or why. The script will often have characters attempt to explain, but frustratingly they do so whilst the much stronger visual language tries to translate the same thing. The famous storytelling rule is to "show not tell", but *Tales from Earthsea* doubles down, deciding to do both. It's frustrating, as the clog of plot overstuffs the joy of the animation.

If the story can be set aside, there is a lot to enjoy in the film, and there's certainly a lot of Ghibli in it. A sequence of farming, rewarded by food, recalls the ethics of hard work and reward found in *My Neighbour Totoro* and *Spirited Away*. A haunting acapella song is akin to Pazu's trumpet solo from *Castle in the Sky*, and the final location – a spindly gothic castle – could have had the same architect as the one found in Hayao Miyazaki's pre-Ghibli film *Lupin III: The Castle of Cagliostro*. Even if the film began with patricide, Gorō Miyazaki actually kept his father alive. Just.

**Opposite:** Hug it out: Goro Miyazaki and his father may have been at loggerheads for his debut feature, but his future films at Ghibli would be closer collaborations.

**Above:** Got to get Therru this. In the finale of the film Therru reveals herself as a dragon.

# PONYO (GAKE NO UE NO PONYO, 2008)

## MIYAZAKI ON SEA

DIRECTED BY HAYAO MIYAZAKI
WRITTEN BY HAYAO MIYAZAKI
LENGTH: 1HR 41MIN
RELEASE DATE (JAPAN): 19 JULY 2008

*HOWL'S MOVING CASTLE* HAD CONTINUED HAYAO MIYAZAKI'S HOT STREAK AT THE JAPANESE BOX OFFICE, AND THE DIRECTOR'S NEXT PROJECT WOULD PROVE TO BE AN AMBITIOUS ABOUT-TURN. PRODUCER TOSHIO SUZUKI RECALLS SUGGESTING THAT MIYAZAKI FOLLOWED THE DARK AND CONFLICTED *HOWL'S MOVING CASTLE* WITH A FILM AIMED SQUARELY AT YOUNGER CHILDREN. WHERE ONCE MIYAZAKI SPENT ONLY A MATTER OF MONTHS MULLING OVER THE PREPARATION FOR HIS FILMS, THE PRE-PRODUCTION FOR *PONYO* SIMMERED AWAY FOR ALMOST TWO YEARS, AS HE SOUGHT INSPIRATION AND FOUGHT THROUGH WAVES OF ARTIST'S BLOCK.

According to Suzuki, part of this came from the prospect of returning to similar territory to Miyazaki's landmark 1988 animation, *My Neighbour Totoro*:

"*Totoro* became Miyazaki's enemy. Nothing Miyazaki made could ever top *Totoro*. This became an obsession. That's why creating *Ponyo* was such a struggle."

*Ponyo*, an onomatopoeic name described by Miyazaki as denoting a "kind of soft, squishy softness", was just one part of the puzzle slowly pieced together over the film's two-year gestation period. Miyazaki was inspired by Hans Christian Andersen's classic fairy tale *The Little Mermaid*, as well as the landscape of the Seto Inland Sea region in Southern Japan, specifically the port town of Tomonoura, which the director visited a number of times for research.

A trip to the UK, and specifically the Tate Britain gallery in London, dramatically changed Miyazaki's perspective on his artistic process. On viewing the work of the pre-Raphaelites, such as Sir John Everett Millais' *Ophelia*, he was struck by attention to detail and use of light. "At that point it became clear to me," Miyazaki remarks in the documentary miniseries *10 Years with Hayao Miyazaki*. "Our animation style could not go on as before."

For his production sketches, Miyazaki used softer pencils and pastels, favouring clean lines over the intricate detail used in the past. While Ghibli is lauded the world over as a bulwark of 2D animation, excelling in the face of the 3D innovations of Disney and Pixar, CG embellishments had crept

**Opposite:** Boy meets fish-girl. The friendship between Sosuke and Ponyo is Ghibli joy at its most pure.

**Below:** "It's haaaaam!" In *Ponyo*, instant ramen becomes a nourishing Ghibli delicacy.

into Miyazaki's films from *Princess Mononoke*, through *Spirited Away*, to *Howl's Moving Castle*. *Ponyo*, in contrast, would be entirely hand-drawn. "Pure realists without dreams are a dime a dozen." Miyazaki remarked. "We must be idealistic realists."

Clearly in an inspired mood, Miyazaki wrote about his "hidden intent" to revolutionise 2D animation in his director's statement for *Ponyo* in June 2006, laying out plans to experiment with, and depart from, the Ghibli house style: decreasing the detail in character designs, but increasing the number of drawings in animating movement; getting rid of straight lines and using "gently warped lines that allow the possibility of magic to exist"; and using simple drawings that "feel warm and liberate the viewer".

Unsurprisingly, this resulted in an intense and dense production process. The resulting film would be made up of 170,000 hand-drawn frames, a record for a Miyazaki film. The director would draw a significant proportion of those frames himself, particularly the scenes involving the ocean, or the waves that Miyazaki was so keen to transform into characters in their own right.

An undeniable visual marvel, *Ponyo* was also another runaway hit for Studio Ghibli. While it didn't make as much as Miyazaki's previous three films, *Ponyo* was the highest-grossing film in Japan in 2008 by far, doubling the takings of the film in second place (live-action romance manga adaptation *Hana Yori Dango Final*), and grossing three times that of its closest Hollywood competitor, *Indiana Jones and the Kingdom of the Crystal Skull*.

The *Indiana Jones* connection is key because *Ponyo*'s release in the US by Walt Disney Pictures was overseen by *Indy* producers Kathleen Kennedy and Frank Marshall. Kennedy and Marshall were no strangers to Ghibli: when I interviewed Kennedy in 2012, she recalled showing Miyazaki's films to her children from a young age, and described him as "the most extraordinary animation talent in the world", adding a unique spin on the "Japanese Disney" moniker by referring to Miyazaki as "the Steven Spielberg of animation".

According to Toshio Suzuki, he had been friends with Kennedy for years, and approached her with the task of cracking the American market after the weak performances of

INSPIRED TO SHAKE UP GHIBLI'S PRODUCTION PROCESS, HAYAO MIYAZAKI RECOMMITTED TO HAND-DRAWN ANIMATION FOR THE CGI-FREE PONYO, AND PERSONALLY CONTRIBUTED TO A CONSIDERABLE CHUNK OF THE FILM'S 170,000 FRAMES.

Ghibli's films in the years since the landmark Disney distribution deal in the 1990s. Kennedy and Marshall enlisted Melissa Mathison, writer of *E.T. the Extra-Terrestrial*, to work on the English-language screenplay, and collaborated with John Lasseter and his team at Pixar to assemble another starry voice cast, including Tina Fey, Liam Neeson, Lily Tomlin, Matt Damon and Cate Blanchett, as well as members of two child-star dynasties, Frankie Jonas and Noah Cyrus, who would voice the young leads Sōsuke and Ponyo.

Released on 927 screens across the US in 2009, *Ponyo* grossed a respectable, if not spectacular, $15 million dollars. It was, without a doubt, the best performing Ghibli film in the US up to that point, but Suzuki's dreams of Miyazaki-mania in America would continue to be unrealized. Outside of Japan and key Asian markets, the Studio's films remained cult favourites. Beloved by fans, it was unlikely to conquer the global box office and rise to the level of the *Harry Potter* franchise or Pixar's *Up* – the latter of which would take home the Academy Award for Best Animated Feature the following year, winning in a category of nominees from which *Ponyo* was conspicuously absent.

**Previous spread:** *Ponyo's* sumptuous, sketchy, hand-drawn vistas are a testament to the talents of Ghibli's artists – such as longstanding background designer Kazuo Oga.

**Above:** After dipping a toe in the waters of CG, Hayao Miyazaki plunged Ghibli back into hand-drawn animation with *Ponyo*.

**Opposite:** Out of the sea, wishing she could be part of that world. Sosuke joins Ponyo in peering at the underwater home she escaped.

**Right:** A ship sails in the Seto Inland Sea, the region of Japan that inspired the setting of *Ponyo*.

*Ponyo* doesn't just wash over you, you swim in it. It is a tidal wave of Ghibli creation. It may initially seem like slight children's stuff, but the dedication of the animators, the vision of the storytelling and the imagination in its sound do more than tell a literal fish-out-of-water story. They bring joy to life.

It may have been an endurance test but the results of Ghibli's hand-drawn style on this film place it in the top tier of their artistic achievements. A wordless opening sequence, featuring the fish Ponyo escaping from her wizard father's submarine domain, is an immensely propulsive action sequence and as colourfully expressive as *Fantasia*. On the surface, shapes and colour are experimented with, pushing Ghibli's style into inventive new territory. A flatter approach to design, with thicker outlines and block colours, makes for clean, bold foregrounding of character and action. In the background, hills and towns are softly sketched with crayon, as if to invite young viewers into a world of their own.

After crashing into the human world – via a garbage trawler that reminds us what damage humans do to her underwater home – Ponyo meets a young boy named Sōsuke, licks some blood on his finger and starts to become human. This unfortunately also creates a drastic tear in the balance of nature, causing immense tidal disasters, which can only be stopped when Ponyo settles as a species again. Written down, the plot suggests that this is all standard fairy-tale stuff, yet it's anything but. In fact, the typical fairy-tale trope of travelling to a magical world, a secret location or down a rabbit hole is inverted, and the magical world is our own. Seen through Ponyo's fresh eyes, life in Sōsuke's small harbour town makes for back-flip inducing levels of excitement, and the only thing that could improve it? Ham!

Ponyo loves ham. And Ponyo loving ham makes for a favourite Ghibli food moment. After coming in from the cold, Sōsuke's mother Lisa makes her son and his new fish-human friend some instant ramen. She pours boiling water into bowls of noodles, then covers them, like a magician hiding the secrets of their great trick. Then abracadabra. There it is, glistening with fat and garnished with greens, eggs and ham, the warming, comforting, most satisfying-looking ramen bowl of your dreams. To the screeching Ponyo, this everyday dish truly is magic and to most viewers of the film it probably is as well.

In another jubilant sequence, Ponyo runs on top of waves to chase down Sōsuke and Lisa's car. Under her magical feet, the waves are transformed into whale-like lifeforms, so powerful is her verve for life that it seems to spring from her every step. As she bounces from wave to wave, Joe Hisaishi's score – which to this point has rivalled *My Neighbour Totoro* for its ebullience – twists into a version of 'Ride of the Valkyries'. It is a giddy moment of pleasure, as Ponyo's beaming happiness contrasts with the crashing waves and orchestra, instantly stealing Wagner's composition from attack helicopters in *Apocalypse Now* and claiming it for herself.

As Ponyo spends more time as a hybrid species, the imbalance of nature grows and great waves that would rival Hokusai cover the town, curiously dredging up elegant, giant, ancient fish into its swell. Caught in the chaos is Lisa – Sōsuke's mother and perhaps the most hilariously reckless driver ever put to animation – who is working at a care home, filled with characterful, lively older women, who also face tidal disasters surprisingly coolly. Lisa is passionate, loving, empathetic (it wouldn't be a surprise to find Kiki or Fio from *Porco Rosso* in her family tree) and, unlike so many grinch-like adults in children's films, she is trusting. It's a trait shared by most of the grown-ups in the film, so when Ponyo and Sōsuke travel across the flooded town by boat to find Lisa, they are refreshingly offered good wishes and support in their intrepid journey from passers-by. Miyazaki's films are often inspiring calls to adventure for the young and in *Ponyo* he tactfully reminds the older viewers to help shepherd that spirit too.

As the stakes and the water rise, any emotional connection to the wider apocalyptic event unfortunately drifts by the wayside, but only because the story of Ponyo and Sōsuke is so strong – even the end of the world pales in comparison to their bond. Thankfully nature's balance is restored, the tide recedes and after a gleeful kiss to end things the credits roll, leaving every viewer as happy as a Ponyo with some ham. Now, where's the nearest ramen shop?

THE GORGEOUS CRAYON-AESTHETIC OF *PONYO'S* JAPANESE POSTER WAS SMOOTHED OUT FOR ITS AMERICAN RELEASE, WITH A POSTER (SEEN BEHIND MIYAZAKI ON PAGE 141) THAT WAS MORE IN-KEEPING WITH THE DISNEY STYLE, LOOKING VERY SIMILAR, IN FACT, TO THE ARTWORK FOR PIXAR'S *FINDING NEMO*.

**Opposite:** The Japanese-language poster for *Ponyo*.

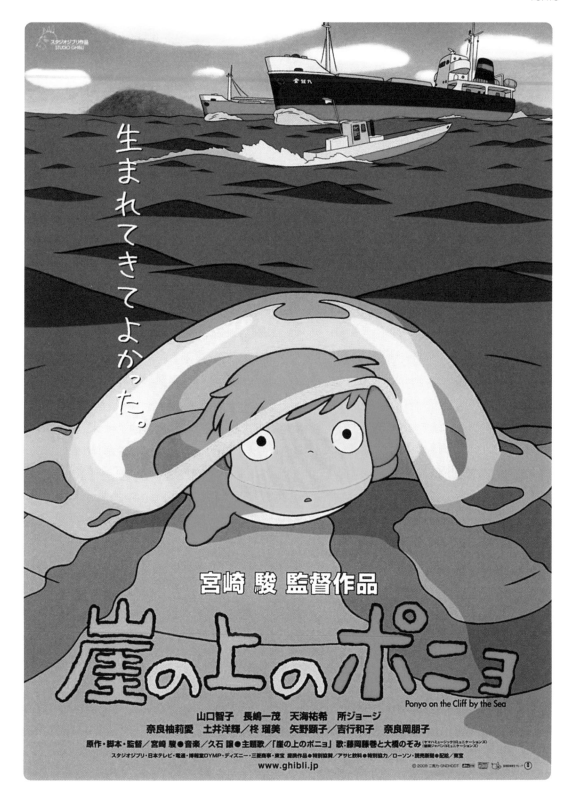

# ARRIETTY
# (KARI-GURASHI NO ARIETTI, 2010)

## THE SECRET WORLD OF
## HIROMASA YONEBAYASHI

DIRECTED BY HIROMASA YONEBAYASHI
WRITTEN BY HAYAO MIYAZAKI & KEIKO NIWA
LENGTH: 1HR 34MIN
RELEASE DATE (JAPAN): 17 JULY 2010

AFTER THE BOX-OFFICE SUCCESS OF *PONYO*, HAYAO MIYAZAKI APPROACHED PRODUCER TOSHIO SUZUKI WITH A FIVE-YEAR PLAN. MIYAZAKI WOULD STEP BACK FROM BEING A HANDS-ON DIRECTOR AND INSTEAD ADOPT MORE OF A "PLANNING-PRODUCER" ROLE, ALLOWING YOUNGER FILMMAKERS TO TAKE UP THE REINS ON A FEATURE FILM PROJECT EACH. THESE TWO PROJECTS WOULD BECOME *FROM UP ON POPPY HILL*, WRITTEN BY MIYAZAKI AND DIRECTED BY HIS SON, GORŌ, AND *ARRIETTY*, A PROJECT BASED ON *THE BORROWERS* BY MARY NORTON.

Reportedly, both Miyazaki and Isao Takahata had considered adapting *The Borrowers* for years, but the role of director for this would fall to 36-year-old Ghibli veteran Hiromasa Yonebayashi. A well-liked member of the Ghibli staff, Yonebayashi, often referred to by the nickname "Maro", provided key animation for several of Miyazaki's shorts and features, starting with *Spirited Away*. He recalls that the first frame he drew on that project featured Chihiro's dad wolfing down a plate of spring rolls.

However, his promotion from animator to director didn't come from his mentor, Miyazaki, but from Toshio Suzuki, who saw potential in the young staffer. Suzuki would describe him as "Ghibli's best animator", but a reluctant director. When Miyazaki and Suzuki offered him the job, he was "thrown for a loop... the thought of directing had probably never entered his mind".

Proving to be more of an ego-free "stage manager"-type than a distinctive, didactic auteur like Hayao Miyazaki, Yonebayashi was perfectly suited for a project like *Arrietty*, which would be scripted by Miyazaki in collaboration with Keiko Niwa (returning to Ghibli fifteen years after she wrote *Ocean Waves*). The young director was given a degree of autonomy, though, when it came to the storyboarding process; Suzuki even saw fit to set him up with an office of his own, away from Miyazaki's prying eyes.

It's all well and good that Miyazaki himself proposed to hand over directing duties to the younger generation, but as

**Opposite:** The face of a new generation. *Arrietty* marks the feature debut of director Hiromasa Yonebayashi.

**Below:** Whatever the size of its characters, *Arrietty* was far from a small-scale Ghibli production.

人間に見られてはいけない。

借りぐらしの
アリエッティ

志田未来　神木隆之介　大竹しのぶ　竹下景子　三浦友和　樹木希林

企画・脚本●宮崎 駿　原作●メアリー・ノートン「床下の小人たち」(林 容吉訳・岩波少年文庫刊)　脚本●丹羽圭子
監督●米林宏昌　音楽・主題歌●セシル・コルベル「Arrietty's Song」

●スタジオジブリ・日本テレビ・電通・博報堂DYMP・ディズニー・三菱商事・東宝・ワイルドバンチ　提携作品●MS&ADホールディングス(三井住友海上・あいおい損保・ニッセイ同和損保)
特別協力●ローソン・読売新聞　配給●東宝

**karigurashi.jp**

we well know by now, in practice the transition of power has never been smooth. A promotional interview that, bafflingly, was included on the *Arrietty* DVD and Blu-ray release sees Miyazaki playing up to the camera in full-blown grump mode, using the forum of promoting a protege's directorial debut to vent spleen: "I had envisaged that we'd produce a lot of new talent," Miyazaki opines, cigarette in hand. "People who were ambitious and had an inexhaustible supply of ideas. But we haven't. So we assigned the job to Maro, who just stood there vacantly." A flash of a grin, a sly look off-camera to where Suzuki is sitting. "Am I being too honest? He's a good guy, but that alone won't produce a good film. There's no use flattering him. As you can see, he's not suited to dealing with the public. We'd rather hide him, not let him wander around."

Competition makes for good copy and perhaps Suzuki isn't above fomenting a bit of intergenerational tension if it helps bolster the box office, but when it comes to Yonebayashi's interview, the wounds run deep. The director remembers starting work at Ghibli and being starstruck by the world-famous Miyazaki – at least until he was called over and given an earful, almost to the point of tears: "His words can pierce you right through to the heart."

Whether this promotional pantomime had an effect or not, *Arrietty* performed well at the box office in 2010,

although it didn't quite scale the blockbusting heights of Miyazaki's own films. By the end of the year, it was the third highest-grossing film in Japan, behind Tim Burton's *Alice in Wonderland* and Pixar's *Toy Story 3* (which, coincidentally, featured a cameo from Totoro). Where Yonebayashi's debut succeeded far beyond the films of his mentor, though, was in the US. Retitled *The Secret World of Arrietty* and given an unprecedented (for Ghibli) 1,500-screen release by Disney, the film grossed just shy of $20 million. Pocket change for the likes of Disney and Pixar, perhaps, but for Ghibli, *Arrietty* (in 2021) still stood as the Studio's highest-grossing film in America. With the exception of *The Wind Rises*, all future Ghibli films would receive modest, targeted US theatrical releases by the animation-focused distributor GKIDS, a company more attuned to the Studio's prestige status in anime, world cinema and the arthouse circuit, and less concerned with producing a blockbuster.

**Above:** On the shoulders of giants. Arrietty (and director Hiromasa Yonebayashi) have to navigate a world previously commanded by large characters.

**Opposite:** The Japanese-language poster for Arrietty.

*Arrietty* changes depending on how you look at it. It can be viewed as a minor work within Ghibli's great library, but it's also their most successful on an international scale, which is no minor achievement. It could be seen to rest on the familiarity of the studio's past creations, but it can also be viewed as a technical progression that pushes it forward. Like the tiny Borrower *Arrietty*, director Hiromasa Yonebayashi is a young person, thrown into a big, new world and both metaphorically, and literally, they both have to deal with new perspectives.

The film begins in well-trodden Ghibli ground. There is a bright blue sky and greenery. As in *My Neighbour Totoro*, *Only Yesterday* and Yonebayashi's next feature *When Marnie Was There*, we are introduced to a character having a healing escape to the country. And there is, of course, a cat with a sense of adventure. Early on it's clear which studio has crafted this film, but there's also a lot different about it too.

Yonebayashi brings in a live-action quality, perhaps inspired by Isao Takahata's occasional documentary-like gaze, including visual techniques more traditionally reserved for camera-captured imagery, not animation. A shallow depth of field, with focus pulling between planes of action, accentuates the gaps between Arrietty and the objects around her, heightening the size divide between her miniature world and that of the newly arrived human boy Shō. Later in the film there is even a dolly zoom, an effective technique for terror most famously used in *Jaws*, where the foreground and background of an image distort and collapse in on each other. The exaggerated scales of the film are also crafted through the sound of it, it is a world where air coming through a plug socket becomes a rattling wind, or the echo of a clock reverberating

through a kitchen makes it feel like an enormous mountain rage.

The sense of light and colour marks a further step away from the Ghibli palette and a sign of what would come next for the director. Soft pools of light sift over the film, and a more muted, dappled watercolour-feel shades the backgrounds. This understated, cloudier look would become even more beautifully realized in Yonebayashi's next film *When Marnie Was There*. And in another creatively foreshadowing design, the plucky wild Borrower Spiller seems to have shared DNA, or at least the same stylist, as the small creatures in Yonebayashi's short film for Studio Ponoc, *Kanini & Kanino*.

Perhaps leaning too far into all things small scale, the greatest rewards come from Arrietty's simpler interactions with the larger props of the human world, albeit with a palpable lack of drama. Haru, a housekeeper, is used to combat this. She is introduced as the villain of the piece, who will stop at nothing to reveal the secret existence of the Borrowers, but her behaviour is erratic, and her motivations are unclear. Compared to Ghibli's more common approach of antagonist-less stories, her mere existence is surprising, and ultimately disappointing. Despite that blemish, the miniature adventure of *Arrietty* remains a big part of Studio Ghibli's history and one that abides by the studio's spirit of finding magic in the everyday – it just depends on your perspective.

**Opposite:** Shō, don't tell. A friendship is formed between human and "Borrower".

**Left:** In the pantheon of Ghibli cats, *Arrietty* offers us a rare example of an antagonistic, frightful feline villain.

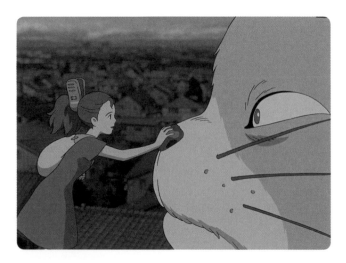

"I SAW MYSELF IN *ARRIETTY* WHEN I WAS MAKING IT," FIRST-TIME DIRECTOR HIROMASA YONEBAYASHI SAID, "BECAUSE SHE HAD TO BORROW THINGS FROM BIG PEOPLE".

# FROM UP ON POPPY HILL
# (KOKURIKO-ZAKA KARA, 2011)

## MIYAZAKI AND SON

DIRECTED BY GORŌ MIYAZAKI
WRITTEN BY HAYAO MIYAZAKI & KEIKO NIWA
LENGTH: 1 HR 31 MIN
RELEASE DATE (JAPAN): 16 JULY 2011

FOLLOWING *ARRIETTY*, THE SECOND FILM IN HAYAO MIYAZAKI'S FIVE-YEAR PRODUCTION PLAN WOULD BE A STYLISTIC CONTRAST. *ARRIETTY* HAD BEEN A FANTASY ADVENTURE IN THE FAMILIAR GHIBLI MOULD, WHILE *FROM UP ON POPPY HILL* IS A HEARTFELT DRAMA LOOSELY BASED ON A GIRLS' MANGA FROM THE EARLY 1980S BY TETSUO SAYAMA AND CHIZURU TAKAHASHI. MIYAZAKI HAD PREVIOUSLY CONSIDERED ADAPTING *FROM UP ON POPPY HILL*, BUT REMAINED UNCONVINCED THAT THE EMOTIONAL LANDSCAPES OF THE GIRLS' *SHOJO* MANGA SUB-GENRE WOULD TRANSLATE EFFECTIVELY TO BIG-SCREEN ANIMATION.

1995's *Whisper of the Heart* had proven otherwise, of course, but it wouldn't be until much later, once the 1960s setting of the manga had gained a more nostalgic power, that *From Up on Poppy Hill* worked its way back into the production slate. Directing duties for *From Up on Poppy Hill* would fall to Gorō Miyazaki, who, after making his divisive debut *Tales from Earthsea* free of any interference or input from his father, would be picking up a project proposed, planned and co-written by him. As with *Arrietty*, Keiko Niwa would write the script with Hayao Miyazaki, and she would be tasked with translating the director's often conflicting creative ideas into a workable form. "This would drive most screenwriters up the wall," producer Toshio Suzuki explains. "But Keiko Niwa found it interesting. She seemed to find his thinking process – the thinking of a genius – immensely intriguing, and she loved working with him.

She was a perfect match for Miya-san."

*From Up on Poppy Hill* was announced to the world as Ghibli's next feature film at a press conference in December 2010, with a release date of July 2011. That plan would be tested by the events following the Tōhoku earthquake and the ensuing nuclear disaster at the Fukushima Daiichi power plant in March 2011. In a press conference following these disasters that affected the full breadth of Japanese society, Hayao

**Above:** Recalling *Whisper of the Heart*, this wholesome moment of a bike ride shared between young lovers is one of *From Up On Poppy Hill*'s most quiet and affecting.

**Opposite:** Croq and roll. Set in the 1960s, the movie is filled with nostalgic cultural reference points from pop music to comfort food.

Miyazaki himself promised that *From Up on Poppy Hill* would
be in cinemas on its proposed release date, saying: "The
postman keeps delivering mail and the bus driver keeps driving
in traffic, so we make a movie."

To hit that deadline, the staff at Ghibli entered crunch mode,
pulling double shifts and dodging rolling blackouts in order to
get the work finished in time. In the end, the film was released
as planned. It fared better with critics than *Tales from Earthsea*,
even picking up Best Animation of the Year at the Japanese
Academy Awards, but while it was the highest-grossing
Japanese film of the year at the domestic box office, its actual
takings were less than half of what *Arrietty* grossed just the year
before. Nevertheless, Suzuki considered this a success, for
not only had the events earlier in the year spoiled the national
appetite for the cinema, Ghibli had also broken with their
expected escapist style for this "risky experiment".

But, of course, the most important opinion of all is that of
Hayao Miyazaki. Footage from the in-house screening of the

finished film is included on the Blu-ray release of *From Up on
Poppy Hill*, and features Miyazaki, firstly, praising the staff for
finishing the film in time ("this is where Ghibli's true strength
lies"), before laying into the film with several searing comments.
"The work has its good parts and not so good parts," he
says. "It turned out to be an immature kind of work." He then
proceeds to lay into the backgrounds, the art style and the
timing and animation of the characters' movement. "I don't
know who made these technical errors, the animator or the
director," he says, as attention inevitably turns to Gorō, "but it is
a very basic mistake."

**Above:** *Characters in* From Up On Poppy
Hill *share a meal. In addition to this one, the
film contains a variety of additions to Ghibli's
lengthy menu of tasty animated moments.*

*From Up on Poppy Hill* is a slight and joyous film, certainly flawed, but made with enormous passion. Whatever his father might say, Gorō Miyazaki's sophomore effort is a success, it is rich in its visual and sonic details, has a loving heart and although it might falter in its narrative, he could only direct the script he was given. The plot, which follows some teenagers as they navigate a blossoming romance and the additional pressure of saving their school clubhouse, may not match the epic scale or intimate fantasy of some of Ghibli's previous work, but if you can find it, there are delights to be found in *From Up on Poppy Hill*'s modest magic.

For Ghibli, *From Up on Poppy Hill* is caught in an era divide, the story shaped by the old master and the execution by the new generation. That same division can be found in the film itself. Set in the transitional Shōwa period, when Japan was embracing more Western culture (characters are even seen drinking Johnnie Walker whisky), Poppy Hill's residents and its surrounding township are both nostalgic and forward-thinking. The students at the story's centre are incredibly passionate and focused on saving their clubhouse, a hub for creative pursuits for generations past, its towering red walls and labyrinthine staircases now crumbling like a geriatric version of the bathhouse from *Spirited Away*. In a pleasing cleaning sequence that similarly echoes *Spirited Away*, the clubhouse is restored to the glory of its former residents, thanks to the prowess and efforts of the new students. In a period of transition for Ghibli, it seems that Hayao Miyazaki's own concerns and goals seeped into his and Keiko Niwa's screenplay.

It is perhaps best to focus on the inspiring clubhouse story when recalling the plot of *From Up on Poppy Hill*, as the romance that dominates the second half of the film, while attempting to reach the highs of *Whisper of the Heart* (including its own romantic bike ride) fails to climb as high. Teenagers Umi and Shun are charming and awkward but their simple romantic rally is interrupted by a convoluted, disarming curveball, as suddenly the threat of possible incest hangs over their blossoming relationship. It's extremely melodramatic – something that the screenplay itself acknowledges – and although it might be a common feature of *shoju* manga, the narrative diversion shifts the film into a jarring high tempo, betraying the superb, gentle first hour.

In another bold (although less controversial) move, one befitting a story of passionate teenagers, *From Up on Poppy Hill* contains Ghibli's most rambunctious soundtrack. The inclusion of pop rock track 'Sukiyaki' by Kyu Sakamoto places us firmly in the early 1960s, and again reflects the trans-Pacific cultural meshing, for as well as a Japanese hit it was also the first non-European-language song to top the US *Billboard* chart. Even more of a highlight is Satoshi Takebe's original score, which outlines the romance plot with swooning soft jazz, and the clubhouse with bombastic, brassy orchestration more befitting of an espionage film than a teen love story. It's a combination of Kenny G and John Barry and, much like the film, is an excellent, unique offering in Ghibli's library.

The richly detailed settings, the lip-smacking food and the adventurous spirit of Ghibli are all here. After the tumultuous process and reception of *Tales from Earthsea*, Gorō Miyazaki didn't exactly step out from his father's shadow with this film, but it no longer looms as large. If the Ghibli clubhouse needs new staff to maintain it, this certifies Gorō as a worthy successor, even if he didn't exactly leave it spotless.

IN HIS DIRECTOR'S NOTES, GORO MIYAZAKI DESCRIBES *FROM UP ON POPPY HILL* AS THE FILM THAT TURNED HIM INTO A FULLY-COMMITTED FILMMAKER. "I DIDN'T WANT TO BE DEFEATED BY MY FATHER'S SCRIPT." HE WROTE. "AS A BOY, I HAD DREAMED OF ANIMATION. BUT WITH MY FATHER THERE IN FRONT OF ME, I HAD GIVEN THAT UP AND BURIED THAT DREAM DEEP INSIDE ME IN MY ADOLESCENT YEARS. I BLAMED THESE TIMES AND MY GENERATION, BUT I MYSELF WAS THE ONE WHO HAD GIVEN UP AND WAS THE COWARD."

**Below:** As Umi and her companions look forward into the future of 20th-century Japan, *From Up On Poppy Hill* sees the rise of a new generation of Ghibli filmmakers.

# THE WIND RISES
# (KAZE TACHINU, 2012)

## BEAUTIFUL, CURSED DREAMS

DIRECTED BY HAYAO MIYAZAKI
WRITTEN BY HAYAO MIYAZAKI
LENGTH: 2HR 6MIN
RELEASE DATE (JAPAN): 20 JULY 2013

FOLLOWING *ARRIETTY* AND *FROM UP ON POPPY HILL*, TWO FILMS DIRECTED BY GHIBLI'S YOUNGER FILMMAKERS, THE CULMINATION OF THE STUDIO'S FIVE-YEAR PRODUCTION PLAN WOULD BE A NEW FILM FROM HAYAO MIYAZAKI. UNPREDICTABLE AS EVER, MIYAZAKI INITIALLY TOYED WITH MAKING A SEQUEL TO *PONYO*, OR AT LEAST A FILM IN A SIMILAR VEIN, BUT PRODUCER TOSHIO SUZUKI HAD OTHER PLANS.

"Working side by side with him for thirty-five years, there was one thing that preyed on my mind," Suzuki writes in *Mixing Work with Pleasure*, referring to a central dichotomy present in the majority of Miyazaki's films:

"He had a detailed knowledge of war-related matters, and loved drawing fighter planes and tanks. On the other hand, he was a great advocate of world peace, and he even participated in anti-war demonstrations. I wanted him to direct a movie that resolved that seeming contradiction."

After delivering *Ponyo*, Miyazaki had returned to his favourite pastime between film projects: drawing manga and illustrated essays for *Model Graphix* magazine. He contributed a story about Jiro Horikoshi, the engineer who designed the Zero fighter aircraft used by the Imperial Japanese Navy in World War II. Like with *Porco Rosso* before it, this series served as the starting point for what would become his next film, *The Wind Rises*.

From 2010, Suzuki urged Miyazaki to adapt the manga into a film, but the director was initially hesitant. He now wanted to make animation for children, something to please his grandson. By 2011, though, he had changed his mind, issuing a project proposal in January that laid out an ambitious plan for a film unique in the Ghibli canon: a historical melodrama with elements of biography, that wrestled with the creative impulses of a genius. "I want to create something that is realistic, fantastic, at times caricatured, but as a whole, a beautiful film," Miyazaki wrote.

"I want to portray a devoted individual who pursued his dream head-on. Dreams possess an element of madness, and such poison must not be concealed. Yearning for something too beautiful can ruin you. Swaying toward beauty may come at a price."

However, *The Wind Rises* isn't a simple biography. The title is taken from a novel by the author Tatsuo Hori, based on his experience of losing his wife to tuberculosis. Miyazaki melds much of Hori's life story with that of Horikoshi, creating a mix of fact and fiction that aims to depict the doomed generation that

**Opposite:** Jiro dreams of flying: the young engineer-to-be fantasises about flying a plane of his own.

**Below:** With their precise drawings and individual desks, perhaps the hard-working Ghibli animators didn't have to look too far to get inspired for this image of aeroplane designers in *The Wind Rises*.

came of age in the 1930s, and their struggle through "an era of recession, unemployment, hedonism and nihilism, war, disease, poverty, modernism and backlash, a march toward the ruin of a stumbling and falling empire".

The making of *The Wind Rises* is covered in intimate detail in Mami Sunada's excellent feature documentary *The Kingdom of Dreams and Madness*, which gives an insight into Miyazaki's struggle through what he would later call a "hellish" production, as doubts and dilemmas started to plague the director's most personal, radical film. The result would be a complex, experimental mix of groundbreaking stylistic flourishes and an almost all-encompassing reassessment of Miyazaki's work to date. Like in *Whisper of the Heart*, everyday scenes were infused with Ghibli magic to reach deeper truths, while an attention to technical, historical and observational detail – from the flush rivets of an aircraft's wing to the precise incline of a polite bow – suggested the methodical, "relentless research" of Isao Takahata.

Figures from the past would return to the fold, too. Steve Alpert, the "resident foreigner" who once sold Ghibli to the

world, was brought out of retirement to lend his likeness and voice to the mysterious character Castorp. Then, mere months before release, after Miyazaki had struggled to pick a voice actor for the role of the reserved, stoic Jiro, an unlikely candidate came to mind: Miyazaki's one-time protégé and *Neon Genesis Evangelion* creator, Hideaki Anno. Almost 30 years after a young Anno wandered into Miyazaki's office with the hopes of landing a job on *Nausicaä of the Valley of the Wind*, they were working together once more.

A planned release date of July 20, 2013 had special resonance. *The Wind Rises* would open in Japanese cinemas twenty-five years after the premiere of *My*

**Above:** With truly nerdy attention to detail, *The Wind Rises* manages to imbue flush rivets and other aspects of engineering with Miyazaki magic.

**Opposite:** The Japanese-language poster for *The Wind Rises*.

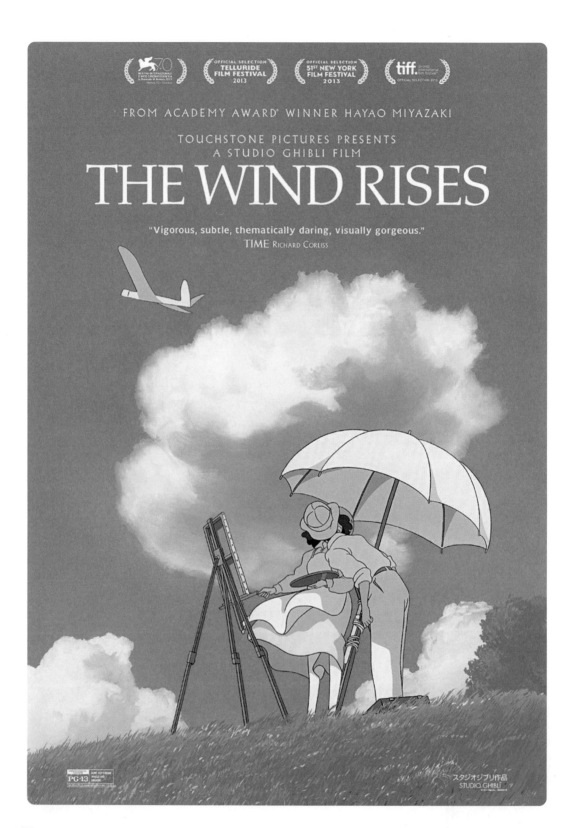

*Neighbour Totoro*. It was initially planned that a new film by Isao Takahata, *The Tale of the Princess Kaguya*, would join it, recreating the 1988 double-bill of *Totoro* and *Grave of the Fireflies*, as both directors neared the end of their careers. According to Toshio Suzuki, the pairing with his old mentor spurred Miyazaki on, while Takahata, as always, preferred to trundle along at his own pace, missing the deadline and leaving *The Wind Rises* to fly on its own.

Any doubts that such serious, weighty material could blunt Miyazaki's box-office hopes were proven to be unfounded. *The Wind Rises* soared at the Japanese box office, comfortably finishing top of the charts at the end of 2013 and becoming one of the highest-grossing Japanese films of all time. Outside of Japan, the film was given the prestige treatment – a premiere in competition at the Venice Film Festival, followed by worldwide theatrical release and an Academy Award nomination –

although the discourse around the film's complex and conflicted politics often overshadowed the work itself.

Also upstaging *The Wind Rises* was Miyazaki himself. On September 4, 2013, days before the Venice premiere, the director announced his retirement from feature filmmaking to focus on other projects, and this time, he seemingly meant it. "I want to continue to work for as long as I can drive and commute back and forth between my home and the Studio," he wrote. "It took five years to complete *The Wind Rises*. Would it take six, or seven even, for the next film? The Studio cannot wait for me, and I will be using up my time in my seventies."

*Princess Mononoke* had once been touted as the culmination of Miyazaki's career, but it is *The Wind Rises* that plays more convincingly as a final masterpiece. To make it, Miyazaki harnessed a lifetime of craft and graft, in order to explore new landscapes of style and meaning. At the staff screening of the finished film, there were tears in his eyes – much to the amusement of Hideaki Anno, who brought up the fact at a press conference and clearly enjoyed making his old mentor squirm.

With *The Wind Rises*, Miyazaki had challenged himself and his chosen medium to create something personal and profound that subverted all expectations associated with Studio Ghibli – and he had succeeded once more. Now, as he wrote in his retirement statement, "I will be free".

**Previous spread:** Dreams: Beautiful but cursed. Jiro's dreams of magnificent, imaginative, aeroplanes make for some of the film's most spectacular sequences. .

**Opposite:** The English-language poster for *The Wind Rises*.

**Below:** The appearance of Giovanni Caproni is meaningful not just for his influential work designing aircraft, but for one plane in particular: the Caproni Ca.309, also known as the Ghibli.

It doesn't have any forest spirits, witches or moving castles but *The Wind Rises* might still be the ultimate Hayao Miyazaki film. Having been constantly fixated with drawing flying machines and having taken that passion and sprinkled it throughout his work at Ghibli, this fictional biopic may be inspired by the lives of plane designer Jiro Horikoshi and author Tatsuo Hori, but it's equally a film about Miyazaki himself.

Primarily taking place in our world in the early twentieth century, with the occasional flight of fancy into the realm of dreams, it's uniquely exciting to watch one of cinema's great fantasy craftsmen operate in reality. The main character of Jiro (a combination of Jiro Horikoshi and Tatsuo Hori) is obsessive and dedicated to his craft of aeroplane design, comparable to Miyazaki not just in the subject of his focus, but in his work. He has an intense attention to detail, conducts relentless working hours and sacrifices time with his family for his profession. He is a born Ghibli animator. When thinking of designs, Jiro's desk hurtles through the sky as if his work itself is the flying machine, and papers whip around him caught in the thrust of his mind. When Miyazaki is in one of his own flights of creativity, one can imagine similar papers strewn around him, catching in the engine of the great animator.

In character Jiro may reflect Miyazaki, but how his craft is shown on screen feels lifted from the textbook of Isao Takahata, in a creative reversal that arguably appears in Takahata's final work, *The Tale of the Princess Kaguya*, as well. The rhythms and minutiae of nature and craft pepper Takahata's work – whether that's the urban development of a western Tokyo suburb in *Pom Poko* or the harvest of safflower in *Only Yesterday* – and in *The Wind Rises* Miyazaki seems inspired by his mentor's essayistic lens in the film's approach to aeroplane design. A continuing fascination with the shape of mackerel bones grips Jiro's imagination until he can use them in a plane design, directly

linking the natural world to that of warfare and satisfying Miyazaki's urge to address his contradicting passions, with a Takahata-esque emphasis on the process of craft. A further investigation into the aerodynamic benefits of deploying flush (as opposed to raised) rivets in the bodywork of a plane is executed with such excitement and satisfaction that it's briefly imaginable to see the planes from Jiro's, Miyazaki's and possibly Takahata's eyes.

These detailed insights into the world of plane manufacture may sound like diversions, but they are key in showing Jiro's knowledge and passion as he reckons with his obsessions, as they tear at both his personal and philosophical ideals. In a surprisingly experimental choice for the director, the linear reality of the story is occasionally broken by Jiro's travels into a dream world of opulent skies, fantastic aircraft and meditations on life, shared with an impressively moustachioed Italian aeroplane designer named Caproni. Like Jiro, Caproni is inspired by a real person, whose work would lead to the creation of the Caproni Ca.309 plane, also known as the "Ghibli". In these conversations the two discuss the contradicting values of their work, Caproni referring to planes as "beautiful, cursed dreams" as they wrestle with the beauty and intricacy of their work, alongside its militarization and power to destroy – at one point in the film Jiro states that one of his ambitious designs could balance its weight issue by removing the guns. Considering Jiro as an avatar for Miyazaki, these conversations can equally be read as an examination of his work in animation, as a discussion between the originator of the Ghibli name and its most prominent standard bearer. While animation may not fire bullets, it certainly dominated Miyazaki's life and perhaps here he questions that.

Although the film interrogates the repercussions of Jiro's obsessions, the romantic figure of Naoko (inspired by the story

of Tatsuo Hori, rather than Jiro Hirokoshi) is unfortunately not developed enough to ever satisfyingly pull the narrative into the argument of his personal life over his professional one. A spectacular imagining of the Great Kanto earthquake, filled with screen-enveloping rippling waves of destruction and terrifying gurgles of flame is the dramatic backdrop for their romantic first meeting, as Jiro carries an injured Naoko through the carnage to safety before disappearing. Years later they reunite at a mountain resort where Jiro is resting after a failed flight test and Naoko has tuberculosis and is convalescing. A playful interaction involving acrobatic paper aeroplanes brings them together with innocent pleasure, but subsequently Naoko is not given much characterization other than her adoration for Jiro. Moments of complex intimacy, like Jiro working in bed still holding hands with the afflicted Naoko

**Above:** Jiro's beloved wife Naoko has the final line in the film, which Miyazaki changed towards the end of production from 'come' to 'live', transforming the film's final moments from a tragic reunion in the afterlife, to a rallying cry to endure through times of hardship.

**Opposite:** Miyazaki's continued interests in nature and flight meet as cows pull one of Jiro's planes.

by his side, are beautifully observed but emotionally distant. Ironically, the director who brought us so many powerful, independent female characters before relegates Naoko to a disappointingly passive muse.

At the end of the film, Jiro and Caproni watch a fleet of Mitsubishi Zeros (Jiro's design masterpiece and a stark image of war) ascend far into the sky to join many other planes in a heavenly convoy. This celestial flightpath is an image Miyazaki also used in *Porco Rosso* and its beauty remains significant, but here, although the blue sky is clear, the message is cloudy. There is no easy reckoning for Jiro's actions; the best he can do, as a vision of Naoko tells him, is to "live".

In *Kiki's Delivery Service*, when the young witch starts her independent life, a radio playing a song by artist Yumi Arai plays on her radio as she triumphantly flies through the air. As the credits roll on *The Wind Rises*, Miyazaki turns to Arai's music again, specifically for a melancholy ode entitled 'Vapour Trail'. These two moments feel like sonic bookends to a career obsessed with flight, from innocently taking off to coming back down to earth, the vapour trails being left behind for us to contemplate the journey.

# THE TALE OF THE PRINCESS KAGUYA (KAGUYA-HIME NO MONOGATARI, 2013)

## THE WATER WHEEL TURNS

DIRECTED BY ISAO TAKAHATA
WRITTEN BY ISAO TAKAHATA & RIKO SAKAGUCHI
LENGTH: 2HR 17MIN
RELEASE DATE (JAPAN): 23 NOVEMBER 2013

EVER THE ELUSIVE, RELUCTANT GENIUS OF STUDIO GHIBLI, ISAO TAKAHATA TOOK FOURTEEN YEARS TO FOLLOW UP 1999'S *MY NEIGHBOURS THE YAMADAS*. WITH THAT FILM, HE HAD ALREADY MOVED AWAY FROM COMMERCIAL FILMMAKING INTO A MORE EXPERIMENTAL REALM, WHERE DEADLINES, BUDGETS AND BOX-OFFICE RECEIPTS BARELY RESONATED IN THE MIND OF THE GREAT DIRECTOR. IT WAS FORTUNATE FOR HIM, THEN, THAT HE, LIKE MANY ARTISTS BEFORE HIM, HAD A BENEFACTOR WILLING TO FUND HIS VISION.

**Above:** With its watercolour textures and pencil-sketch aesthetic, *The Tale of the Princess Kaguya* looks like nothing else in the Ghibli canon.

**Opposite:** In a joyful moment in what is a surprisingly melancholy film, Princess Kaguya dances among pink blossoms. .

Seiichiro Ujiie, chairman of Nippon Television, was a long-time supporter of Studio Ghibli, appearing as a producer on many of their films from *Ocean Waves* onwards, as well as supporting the founding of the Ghibli Museum and commissioning many Ghibli-related exhibitions as part of his role as director of the Museum of Contemporary Art in Tokyo. But, most of all, he was a devoted fan of Takahata, to the extent that he pledged to give the filmmaker the financial support he needed to create another film.

Takahata took his time. Toshio Suzuki says that an adaptation of the samurai epic *The Tale of the Heike* was in the works, but was scrapped when Takahata's preferred animation director, Osamu Tanabe, refused to work on a project filled with scenes of violence. Instead, Takahata returned to a project he first pitched to his superiors at Toei Animation in the early 1960s, an adaptation of the tenth-century folk story *The Tale of the Bamboo Cutter*.

The project began, slowly, in 2005. Long-serving producer Suzuki decided to step back into a "planning" role, initially delegating production duties to his young assistant Taku Kishimoto. Kishimoto, nicknamed "Nayo" by Suzuki, had previously worked on *Tales from Earthsea*, and had pitched to write the screenplay for *Arrietty*, but Hayao Miyazaki had rejected his proposal. Instead, he now had the task of supporting Isao Takahata during pre-production on his new feature project. But Takahata dithered, considering other possible directions and stories before fully committing to *The Tale of the Princess Kaguya*.

Studio Ghibli's president Koji Hoshino announced a new Takahata film was in the works in February 2008, while Takahata himself revealed his plans as he received the Leopard of Honour award at the 2009 Locarno Film Festival. By then, though, Kishimoto had quit Ghibli in order to retrain as a screenwriter; now, his short stint at Ghibli is a mere footnote in a long and successful career that includes writing the popular volleyball anime *Haikyu!!*. Stepping up to the plate next was another young member of Ghibli's editorial team, Yoshiaki Nishimura, who had previously worked on *Howl's Moving Castle* as a production manager. Nishimura was in his mid-twenties when he first joined the project, and by the time *The Tale of the Princess Kaguya* finally reached cinemas, he would be married with two kids, having dedicated a third of his life to supporting Takahata's vision.

Takahata's original screenplay was over three and a half hours long, and the storyboarding process itself took several years. At one point, Nishimura estimated that they were working at a rate of two minutes of screen time a month, such was Takahata's deliberate pace of work. To help matters, Suzuki gave the production its own remote studio, away from the bustle of Ghibli, with a small outsourced staff and a relaxed atmosphere that best complemented its director.

Moving out of Ghibli's primary studio was apt for *The Tale of the Princess Kaguya*, as it would break with almost all conventions associated with the Studio. As with *My Neighbours the Yamadas*, Takahata wanted to experiment with form. He wanted to throw out much of the expected house style of animation and replace it with a sketchy aesthetic that focused on the hand-drawn lines behind every figure, with watercolour backgrounds that bleed into negative white space. When I interviewed Takahata in 2013, he put it this way:

"I often say that with this loose or rough sketch-type drawing, leaving some spaces unfilled allows people to use their imagination. But I also think there's the aspect of conveying the excitement that the artist feels when he's drawing a very quick sketch. So that kind of vitality and liveliness also appears in the film and I really appreciated that."

Capturing something so organic and human in animation required a lot of work. In order to preserve the spirit of the

**Opposite, Above:** A young female character, in flight, synchronised with nature. Is this actually a secret Hayao Miyazaki film?

**Opposite, Below:** Despite sitting in the palace built for her, Princess Kaguya yearns for her previous life that was closer to nature.

**Below:** Isao Takahata (fifth from left) leads a press conference for *The Tale of the Princess Kaguya* as the long-gestating film is completed.

rough sketch, in-between animators would have to trace over the brush strokes of the key animators, precisely mimicking the thickness and softness of their line art in every frame. The result was stunning, but Toshio Suzuki estimated that this method could take up to four times as long as more traditional animation; it would be perfect for an experimental short film, but Takahata was out of his mind to adopt that approach for a feature-length film. Luckily, Takahata had support: animation director Osamu Tanabe and art director Kazuo Oga were up for the challenge, and a five billion yen investment from Seiichiro Ujiie kept the film afloat through a protracted production. Ujiie passed away in 2011; he had wished for another Takahata project to take with him into the afterlife, but in the end he was only able to read the script and see a selection of finished storyboards.

*The Tale of the Princess Kaguya* missed its initial summer 2013 release date, with Nishimura shouldering not just the responsibility of announcing the delay, but also some playful teasing from Suzuki in front of the press. The film would instead reach cinemas in November 2013, where it grossed under half its production budget, making around a fifth of *The Wind Rises'* box office. Internationally, the film was Takahata's first taste of the festival circuit, premiering in the Directors' Fortnight selection in Cannes, opening the Annecy International Animated Film Festival and screening at the Toronto International Film Festival in 2014. *The Tale of the Princess Kaguya* would also be the first, and only, Takahata film to be nominated for an Oscar, losing out in 2015 to Disney's *Big Hero 6*.

Unlike Miyazaki, Takahata never formally retired. *The Tale of the Princess Kaguya* may be marked with the melancholy of

being a final masterpiece, but it stands as a powerful testament to what Takahata sought to achieve in animation. After finishing the project, Takahata worked with Michaël Dudok de Wit as an "artistic producer" on *The Red Turtle*, and further mentored Yoshiaki Nishimura as he set up his own company, Studio Ponoc. Nishimura would later reveal that he'd approached the director with the idea of contributing a short film for Ponoc's *Modest Heroes* anthology, a project permanently shelved by Takahata's death in April 2018.

After the news of Takahata's death circulated, tributes poured in as animators and filmmakers including Aardman Animations' Peter Lord, Pixar's Lee Unkrich, Sylvain Chomet, Tomm Moore and Michel Ocelot all saluted his work and enduring influence. At his funeral, Miyazaki delivered a eulogy that reflected on fifty-five years of friendship, collaboration and competition, and described their first meeting at a very Ghibli-appropriate location: a bus stop in the rain. "I was so glad that I got to encounter a man of such rare intellect," he said.

**Above:** Isao Takahata (left) and producer Yoshiaki Nishimura (right) attend a reception for filmmakers nominated in the Best Animated Feature category at the Academy Awards. Nishimura later formed his own animation company, Studio Ponoc.

**Opposite:** Japanese-language poster for *The Tale of the Princess Kaguya*.

**Previous spread:** In a sequence of vibrant colour and movement, Princess Kaguya gets caught up in the lush fabrics that mark her new royal life, a life that tragically comes to trap her.

*The Tale of the Princess Kaguya* is the film that Isao Takahata spent his lifetime making. It may have begun production in 2008, but from its stylistic references to the imbuing of its creator's relaxed pace, decades of Takahata's unmistakable work culminate in *The Tale of the Princess Kaguya*, forming a perfect artistic epitaph for one of the masters of animation.

It is immediately clear from the first brush stroke that the animation here is something new, there's no Ghibli "house style" but a focus on loose, sketched lines that invigorate every frame with the energy of an inspired artist, rushing to put paint to canvas. Only the essential elements of each frame are created, often leading to considerable blank space around the action, allowing us to both focus on exactly what's important while imagining what else might fill this stunning world. Caught in charcoal lines and watercolour, Takahata and his team don't cover the screen, but it is filled with concentrated emotional texture. The story of a bamboo cutter and the mystical princess he finds in a tree may be a thousand years old, but the vitality of the film's style injects it with palpable urgency.

After discovering the princess, the bamboo cutter and his wife see her age in an instant, slipping from newborn to young adult in moments, the animation elegantly hiding the joins of growth, recollecting in many parental viewers their own experience of the speed and invisibility of watching a child grow up. The rural grove that the family inhabits allows Takahata to explore his continuing fascinations with nature

and agriculture in ways that recall his previous films, while rejuvenating them with new style and thematic weight. A lesson in traditional bowl making is a partner to the safflower harvest from *Only Yesterday*, a bird singing in blossom echoes a very similar image from *My Neighbours the Yamadas* and the cutting of a melon directly revisits the same motion seen in *Grave of the Fireflies* (this is because Takahata actually felt he didn't get it right the first time). As the area is farmed however, the woodland dies and the villagers have to leave to allow nature a fallow decade of recovery, poignantly instilling a sense of cyclical mortality to the film that pervades its entirety.

Although the princess loves her rural home, a further discovery of gold in the bamboo shoots allows her father to build her a palace in the city and move her there, giving her the home he feels she deserves, and subsequently inspiring suitors for his daughter. It's within the trappings of the palace that the melancholia of the film forms more fully as the father and daughter's ideals begin to clash, and this clashing leads Takahata's film to become his most similar to that of his great protégé, Hayao Miyazaki.

Channelling Kiki, Chihiro, San and more, Kaguya fights against the patriarchal regime now forced on her as she yearns for her life back among nature. After being referred to as a treasure, she comedically tasks her suitors with finding mythical (and non-existent) treasures to win her heart, highlighting their objectification of her and the materialism ingrained in

her social escalation. In lessons aimed to teach her about the performance of nobility, in perhaps a nod to the craft that her story is being told in, she draws cartoons instead of arch calligraphy. She revolts against the feminine styles of the time that would have her appear emotionless, her sparks of life continually contrasting with the restrictive and empty palace.

In maybe the most memorable sequence she breaks free, frantically rushing back to the forest, while the animation hopes to keep up with her. The elegant line strokes become a flurry of scratched charcoal and an abstract sketch of Kaguya bounces around the frame, as if trying to escape the telling of her own story.

This expression of frustration contrasts with a later sequence in which Kaguya elegantly starts to fly (recalling Takahata's own *Only Yesterday* again), a reunion with a childhood friend allowing her to emotionally soar rather than thrash, softly gliding around her old home in a joyous flight of nostalgia that rivals the magnificence of any Miyazaki aerial trip.

In the last act of the film, the palace prison, its inhabitants and visitors having become too much, Kaguya despairingly calls out for help. In a late twist, her saviours are revealed to be the beings that magically placed her with the bamboo cutter in the first place, the people of the Moon. Although adapted directly from the original, this addition to the story is slightly jarring and considering the experimentation throughout, some earlier seeding of Kaguya's lunar family could have smoothed out this revelation. Once accepted however, the final moments of the film offer an astounding meditation on life, as Takahata addresses his own mortality. Despite the pain

she discovered as a human, Kaguya ultimately would rather endure that than return to the cold of the moon, which we learn is a place of no emotion. Sat atop a cloud, the Moon people arrive as a spectral parade, like another conjuring from the tanuki of Takahata's *Pom Poko*, accompanied by a jangling, disconcertingly chipper score. It tragically contrasts and heightens the melancholy of Kaguya, but subsequently offers affirmation in the human experience, Takahata assuring us of the value in simply feeling.

*The Tale of the Princess Kaguya* manages to be both a brave new direction and a greatest hits compilation, constantly treading new ground while referencing previous work, as a final directorial work it is the perfect sign off from Takahata. With his own final exit unknowingly lying ahead, in working with young producer Yoshiaki Nishimura he burnishes new talent, not leaving a gap behind but simply a fallow interval, as the cycle of animation lives on.

**Above:** The lush fabrics that once delighted Kaguya come to symbolise the way patriarchal society confines women. When dressed up, she is to be kept indoors to be courted by suitors.

**Opposite:** Centuries old character, the Bamboo Cutter. He also makes an appearance in Takahata's film *My Neighbours The Yamadas*. See page 106 to see Mr Yamada performing the same role.

# WHEN MARNIE WAS THERE (OMOIDE NO MĀNĪ, 2014)

## FINE ON THE OUTSIDE

DIRECTED BY HIROMASA YONEBAYASHI
WRITTEN BY HIROMASA YONEBAYASHI, KEIKO NIWA & MASASHI ANDO
LENGTH: 1HR 42MIN
RELEASE DATE (JAPAN): 19 JULY 2014

WITH *ARRIETTY*, DIRECTOR HIROMASA YONEBAYASHI HAD STOOD UP TO HAYAO MIYAZAKI'S EXAMPLE – AND HIS PLAYFUL TEASING – AND DELIVERED A HIT. HE'D EVEN IMPRESSED THE MASTER HIMSELF: "IT WAS GOOD," MIYAZAKI REPORTEDLY SAID. "I CRIED." FOLLOWING THE FILM'S RELEASE, YONEBAYASHI RETURNED TO HIS ROLE AS ONE OF GHIBLI'S LEADING KEY ANIMATORS, WORKING ON BOTH *FROM UP ON POPPY HILL* AND *THE WIND RISES*, BUT, NO DOUBT BUOYED BY *ARRIETTY*'S SUCCESS, THE FORMERLY RELUCTANT DIRECTOR EVENTUALLY APPROACHED PRODUCER TOSHIO SUZUKI HIMSELF TO FORMALLY REQUEST A SECOND FEATURE TO DIRECT.

Suzuki handed Yonebayashi a copy of Joan G. Robinson's Carnegie Medal-winning 1964 novel *When Marnie Was There*. The novel was a favourite of Hayao Miyazaki's, appearing on the filmmaker's list of 50 recommended children's books, but Suzuki believed Yonebayashi would be the perfect choice for adapting it for the big screen. In his book *Mixing Work with Pleasure: My Life at Studio Ghibli*, Suzuki explained his reasoning:

"[Miyazaki] couldn't make a movie like *Marnie*. [Yonebayashi] was clearly more sensitive than Miya-san, and he was younger. I instinctively felt that this film would have an appeal that differed from Miya-san's fantasy films."

The film would also be focused on two female characters, with no members of the opposite sex to provide conflict, romance or resolution to the plot, something Suzuki thought was "very modern" and played into Yonebayashi's interests: "Just as Miya-san enjoyed drawing fighter planes, Maro [Yonebayashi] probably had a steadfast liking for drawing girls. I was certain that he would enjoy differentiating the two characters."

Suzuki himself would step back from his regular role of producer, instead operating as a general manager putting the

**Above:** A breathtaking example of the "pearl-coloured" skies Hiromasa Yonebayashi wanted to capture in his second feature for Ghibli.

**Opposite:** *When Marnie Was There* rows Ghibli into previously unexplored emotional waters.

right crew members in place. Yoshiaki Nishimura, who had handled production on *The Tale of the Princess Kaguya*, was made producer for *When Marnie Was There*, while animator Masashi Ando, a veteran of projects with Miyazaki (*Princess Mononoke*, *Spirited Away*) and Isao Takahata (*Pom Poko*, *The Tale of Princess Kaguya*) was brought on board as both animation director and character designer. Ando would also collaborate on the screenplay with Yonebayashi and Ghibli stalwart Keiko Niwa.

This gave *When Marnie Was There* the unique honour of being Ghibli's first major theatrical feature not to have direct involvement from either Miyazaki or Takahata. With even Suzuki taking a step back, it seemed that the Studio's desire to hand over the reins to the next generation had finally been realized. In Yonebayashi's words, *Marnie* would have to be made "without help from the giant".

Yonebayashi, Ando and their team approached the film with several key visual ideas that broke the Ghibli mould. Characters' expressions would be more detailed, while the film's countryside setting would be rendered with an almost photorealistic style. The creative team scouted locations in Hokkaido in northern Japan, specifically the region's marshy wetland areas, a terrain that hadn't been depicted before in a Ghibli film. The trademark blue skies and green hills of Miyazaki's films would be replaced with cloudy, murky, nuanced skies with overlapping colours and subtle hues, described by Yonebayashi as "pearl-coloured".

*When Marnie Was There* was released in Japanese cinemas in July 2014, just eight months after the delayed release of *The Tale of the Princess Kaguya*. Something of a disappointment at the box office, the film made only a third of what *Arrietty* grossed in 2010, and by the end of the year only just cracked the list of the top ten highest-grossing Japanese films.

What mustn't have helped its chances with audiences was the announcement in August that Studio Ghibli would go on a production hiatus – a "brief pause" in Suzuki's words – following Miyazaki's retirement after finishing *The Wind Rises*. The retirement would prove to be short-lived, and by 2016 Miyazaki would be back in production on a new feature, *How Do You Live?* – albeit working at a snail's pace that would drag into the next decade.

Undeterred, producer Yoshiaki Nishimura took inspiration from his mentors and struck out on his own. In April 2015, Nishimura founded Studio Ponoc, a new company started from scratch that would continue Ghibli's legacy of high-quality animation that could be enjoyed by adults and children alike.

Nishimura's first feature project would be an adaptation of another English-language children's book, Mary Stewart's *The Little Broomstick*, and he poached Yonebayashi to direct, alongside a production staff stuffed with Ghibli alumni, who would be working at desks literally lifted from one of the older company's shuttered studios.

*Mary and the Witch's Flower*, with its wilful witch-to-be, broomstick in hand and familiar black cat by her side, would have its fair share of nods to the work of both Hayao Miyazaki and Isao Takahata, but Nishimura and Yonebayashi's ambitions lay beyond mere imitation. The studio name is key: taken from the Croatian word for "midnight", it signalled a new day for Japanese animation, much like how Ghibli's evocation of the sirocco winds represented a breath of fresh air blowing through the industry almost thirty years earlier.

**Opposite:** Marnie's Western-style mansion makes a distinct impression in this radical Studio Ghibli feature.

**Below:** Anna and Marnie as seen in character sketches.

あなたのことが大すき。

Découvrez le nouveau grand film d'animation du Studio Ghibli,
par le réalisateur d'ARRIETTY.

# SOUVENIRS DE MARNIE

### Un film de HIROMASA YONEBAYASHI

D'APRÈS LE ROMAN ORIGINAL "WHEN MARNIE WAS THERE" PAR JOAN G. ROBINSON  SCÉNARIO DE KEIKO NIWA  MASASHI ANDO ET HIROMASA YONEBAYASHI
RÉALISÉ PAR HIROMASA YONEBAYASHI  SUPERVISEUR DE L'ANIMATION MASASHI ANDO  CHEF DÉCORATEUR YOHEI TANEDA  MUSIQUE DE TAKATSUGU MURAMATSU
THÈME DE LA CHANSON "FINE ON THE OUTSIDE" INTERPRÉTÉE PAR PRISCILLA AHN  STUDIO GHIBLI  NIPPON TELEVISION NETWORK  DENTSU
HAKUHODO DYMP  WALT DISNEY JAPAN  MITSUBISHI  TOHO ET KDDI PRÉSENTENT UNE PRODUCTION STUDIO GHIBLI "WHEN MARNIE WAS THERE"
PRODUCTEUR EXÉCUTIF EN CHEF TOSHIO SUZUKI  PRODUCTEUR EXÉCUTIF KOJI HOSHINO  PRODUIT PAR YOSHIAKI NISHIMURA

スタジオジブリ作品
STUDIO GHIBLI

wild bunch

©2014 GNDHDDTK

FRENETIC

# REVIEW: WHEN MARNIE WAS THERE

After being sent to the country in an attempt to aid her anxious mind, the teenage Anna arrives at her relatives' home and immediately, unconsciously places her bag on top of an engraving of the word "love", the word now hidden from her. It's a gesture indicative of the murky, awkward, previously unexplored emotions that Ghibli tackles in this film. Anna is closed off to the world, not precocious but insular; she is self-loathing and would be considered more of an outsider, than independent. She is not a typical Ghibli protagonist, and *When Marnie Was There* is not a typical Ghibli film.

Anna suffers from an anxiety attack at the start of the film, notable not only for Ghibli exploring mental health in a nuanced, understanding way, but because it happens when Anna attempts to share the work she's been doing in her sketchbook. She is an artist and an artist of Yonebayashi's sensibilities rather than Miyazaki's. The notoriously cold Miyazaki is not as expressive or emotional as his young protégé: in the Miyazaki-penned *Whisper of the Heart*, art is a craft that is honed over a long time and developed, and for Yonebayashi it is an emotional, creative expression that carries the weight of vulnerability. Anna's anxieties live on her page and when she attempts to share them, she is rejected and spirals downwards, a rock bottom that starts her journey.

This is a Ghibli film, so of course heading into nature is always a useful cure for any ailment and it is out in the marshland of Hokkaido that Anna starts to understand herself more. Kissakibetsu, the small seaside town that Anna travels to, is stunningly rendered. The realist style finds Ghibli's love of nature at its most tangible, the surrounding forest grazes the arm, the marsh squishes underfoot and the fresh sea air drifts through the screen. The pearlescent skies do away with the crisp, comfortable Ghibli blue, often beautifully reflected in the sea water, the colourful gradients and gloomy greys a fitting and more realistic frame for the tumult of adolescence. When Anna stands at the edge of the water, she looks across the marsh and sees a grand house in a pocket of light, and in the window is a young girl she'll come to know, called Marnie.

Marnie and Anna spark up an intimate and intense friendship. Both young women have deep sadness within them. While Anna's noticeably fractures her social interactions, Marnie's issues of abandonment, stemming from abuse in her pristine home, remain buried under a gleeful appearance, and together they intuit a profound connection. A paired boat ride across the sunset pink lake, complete with *Titanic*-style posing and professions of adoration, is achingly romantic, but tragically it cannot be. Not because society won't accept their relationship, but because despite even the film's own idyllic presentation of them, they are not a couple. Of course, Marnie is in fact a ghost, the ghost of Anna's grandmother.

It is not a completely bewildering decision, as the intergenerational relationship explains their miraculous, almost spiritual affinity for one another, but having already negotiated a possible familial romance a few years earlier in *From Up on Poppy Hill*, it's certainly a surprise. As with that film, the third act is not where *When Marnie Was There* shines. It is perhaps Ghibli's most emotional film, not because it's the one to make you shed the most tears (that crown will always belong to *Grave of the Fireflies*), but because it is so full of feeling. Lost or confused viewers will find reassurance in the film's young leading pair, just as they might find inspiration in Kiki or Nausicaä. Like most teenagers, Anna and Marnie experience the world with great intensity, both the light and the dark, and all the gradients in between.

**Left:** *When Maro Was There*. Director Hiromasa Yonebayashi was given the nickname "Maro" by his colleagues.
**Opposite:** The French-language poster for *When Marnie Was There*.

# THE RED TURTLE
# (LA TORTUE ROUGE, 2016)

### EURO-GHIBLI

DIRECTED BY MICHAËL DUDOK DE WIT
WRITTEN BY MICHAËL DUDOK DE WIT, PASCALE FERRAN
LENGTH: 1 HR 21 MIN
RELEASE DATE (JAPAN): 17 SEPTEMBER 2016

FEWER THAN TWO YEARS AFTER TOSHIO SUZUKI ANNOUNCED THE "BRIEF PAUSE" IN PRODUCTION AT STUDIO GHIBLI, THE UNMISTAKABLE TOTORO LOGO GRACED THE BIG SCREEN AT THE CANNES FILM FESTIVAL'S DEBUSSY THEATRE IN 2016. ONLY THIS TIME, INSTEAD OF THE ICONIC GHIBLI BLUE, IT WAS COLOURED RED.

*The Red Turtle* was hardly the first time Ghibli had co-produced a project – most notably, the Studio had lent its cultural heft to help Mamoru Oshii raise the budget for *Ghost in the Shell 2: Innocence* – but that logo was significant. As was the presence of producers Isao Takahata and Toshio Suzuki, both supporting the film and director Michaël Dudok de Wit during its international premiere as part of Cannes' *Un Certain Regard* selection.

Dutch-born, but London-based, Dudok de Wit had won the Academy Award for Best Animated Short Film in 2001 for the beautiful *Father and Daughter*, and it was in 2006, when the team at the Ghibli Museum enquired about distributing the short in Japan, that a second suggestion was raised: that he work with Studio Ghibli on a feature film. Fully aware of how difficult it is to find financing and production support for feature-length animated films, Dudok de Wit was attracted by Ghibli's offer. "I remember thinking: 'If ever there was a time to make a feature film, this was it.' They make director's films."

The project would be produced by Toshio Suzuki, Isao Takahata (serving as "artistic" producer) and Vincent Maraval of the French distributor Wild Bunch. As he developed the script, Dudok de Wit would meet with Takahata and Suzuki in both Japan and France, where the film would be produced. It was out of these discussions with Takahata that the most radical creative suggestion came: doing away with speech and making the film dialogue-free.

*The Red Turtle* picked up a special prize at Cannes and was eventually nominated for Best Animated Feature at the Academy Awards in 2017. If you put it in a line-up of Ghibli's productions, it might stick out like, well, a giant red turtle, but the project stands as both a tribute to an integral European influence on Studio Ghibli that often goes unremarked, but also a testament to Takahata's wisdom as a filmmaker. Recalling their collaboration, Dudok de Wit told the British Film Institute:

"It was the most wonderful experience working with Takahata... Over and over again I was aware of his wise intelligence and his strong intuition. Listening to him, it was obvious that I was in the presence of a great master."

**Opposite:** Face to fate. The man confronts the titular turtle.

**Below:** Synchronised swimming. The Boy and the turtles glide through the water.

Make no mistake, *The Red Turtle* is a Studio Ghibli film. The red logo at the start might suggest it's something else, but the gently absorbing confines of this seemingly simple desert island story contain clear Ghibli genealogy, and if you travel to it, you'll discover a masterpiece. It is a survival story about dying. The life of a perfectly anonymous man, from terrifying first gasps for breath, to contented final ones. He isn't trapped, he is merely a human being given the great task of being alive. Unlike most desert island stories, what makes *The Red Turtle* great is that it's not about escaping.

The cast list might be small, but the story is teeming with life, life that is given the admiration that we come to expect from Ghibli. In a flatter yet precise style compared to other Ghibli films, fish, crabs, lizards, frogs and millipedes all make beautiful appearances – even a bat appears, and in maybe a first for its kind, is not seen to be scary in any way. And there is, of course, the turtle. First encountered when destroying the man's makeshift rafts, hidden beneath the waves, it is perceived to be dangerous. But when it is shown, resting in the blue frame of the ocean, it reveals its stunning elegance, staring deeply into the man's eyes and filling the screen, as if to declare the inevitability of its presence.

When the turtle washes up on shore the man attacks it, and because of the delicate treatment the island's creatures have been given earlier (and what we expect from the Studio), this act of violence is incredibly shocking. But he is thrashing out at fate, at the stalking embodiment of it, unaware of the joys it can hold. When the shell cracks open, it feels like a splitting glacier from a disaster film, but it's not a cataclysmic event that follows, it's something far bigger and far more intimate, it is a family.

The magic of nature provides. A woman appears from the turtle and joins the man in his life on the island, at first she is understandably reserved, but they commune in that most Ghibli of ways: over food. It is one of the Studio's most touching food moments, because of touch. The woman collects mussels, prepares them and gives one to the man – it is the tactility of nourishment, reflecting their growing intimacy.

The pair are soon joined by a son and the joys and terrors of the island become more extreme, as the parents view their surroundings through the lens of their boy, feelings that are expertly conveyed through Laurent Perez Del Mar's exquisite score. Although the setting might be small, Del Mar's orchestration is as sizable and layered as one could hope for a parable about an entire life experience. The joyful patter of tiny feet on a beachside walk, the threat of drowning, the pride and heartbreak of flying the nest (or swimming from the island), and even death all echo perfectly through delicate plucked strings and enormous bows.

In a scene of destruction, only rivalled by the firebombing in *Grave of the Fireflies* and the earthquake in *The Wind Rises*, the island is wiped of almost all its life by a tidal wave. It is disorienting as water, plants and people clatter across the screen. But, even on the other end of an apocalyptic event, the family survives and despite their losses they emerge just as strong. Basking in a golden light, offsetting the debris of the worst of life, they are together and together they share some food.

**Above:** See wall. In one of the film's most memorable visuals, a huge wave becomes frozen in time.

THE JAPANESE-LANGUAGE POSTER FOR THE RED TURTLE. BEWARE: THE FRENCH-LANGUAGE POSTER, USED FOR THE FILM'S CANNES PREMIERE AND LATER THEATRICAL RELEASE, CONTAINS A SIGNIFICANT PLOT SPOILER.

# EARWIG AND THE WITCH
# (ĀYA TO MAJO, 2020)

## GHIBLI ENTERS THE THIRD DIMENSION

DIRECTED BY GORŌ MIYAZAKI
WRITTEN BY KEIKO NIWA & EMI GUNJI
LENGTH: 1HR 22MIN
RELEASE DATE (JAPAN): 30 DECEMBER 2020 (TV)

STUDIO GHIBLI – FOR MANY THE LAST BASTION OF TRADITIONAL, HAND-DRAWN ANIMATION – HAD LONG BEEN CAUTIOUS ADOPTERS OF DIGITAL TECHNOLOGY. AS WE HAVE SEEN, KEY COMPUTER-ASSISTED TECHNIQUES HAD CREPT INTO THE GHIBLI ANIMATION PROCESS FROM THE 1990S ONWARDS, BUT THE STUDIO ALWAYS MAINTAINED THAT THEY WERE FIRST AND FOREMOST 2D ANIMATORS, NOT, LIKE THEIR PEERS AT PIXAR, INTERESTED IN PURSUING THE ART OF 3DCG ANIMATION.

It's well documented that Hayao Miyazaki himself was a fierce skeptic, as seen in the 2016 documentary *Never-Ending Man: Hayao Miyazaki*, which not only finds the old master struggling to incorporate CG animation into the production of his 2018 short film *Boro The Caterpillar*, but also features a now-notorious scene in which representatives from a tech company demonstrate a new system that should, in theory, generate lifelike animation without the need for an artist's hand. Miyazaki's withering reaction has since become an omnipresent meme: "I strongly feel that this is an insult to life itself."

Meanwhile, Ghibli's other Miyazaki was well on his way to embracing 3DCG. 2014 saw the premiere of *Ronja, the Robber's Daughter*, a 3D-animated TV series co-produced by Ghibli and directed and storyboarded by Goro Miyazaki. The experience was clearly a positive one, as Goro's next feature would, against all expectations, be Ghibli's first 3DCG feature.

The announcement of *Earwig and the Witch* in 2020 came as nothing short of a surprise. Interest in Ghibli was at a peak after their library had been released globally on the streaming services Netflix and HBO Max, while tantalizing news of both Hayao Miyazaki's feature *How Do You Live?* and the long-mooted Ghibli theme park kept fans daydreaming of a near-distant future. Little did they know that a new feature was already fully finished, and ready to launch.

Developed and produced behind closed doors, *Earwig and the Witch* was suggested for adaptation by Hayao Miyazaki, who came across the source novel, a short posthumous work by *Howl's Moving Castle* author Diana Wynne Jones, when browsing in a bookshop. Producer Toshio Suzuki tapped Goro for the project, and suggested, following *Ronja*, that this could be an ideal project for 3D animation. The board was set. *Earwig and the Witch* featured input from a few key Ghibli veterans (Katsuya Kondō contributed character designs, while Keiko Niwa co-wrote the screenplay and Satoshi Takebe composed the score), but it was predominantly animated by a young and international staff working with the studio for the first time.

Goro Miyazaki has never had much luck when it comes to outside forces disrupting his films. His debut *Tales From Earthsea* was overshadowed by his father's legacy, while *From Up On Poppy Hill* had to be produced through the rolling

blackouts following the Fukushima disaster in 2011. Then, in the COVID-19-impacted landscape of 2020, with cinemas shuttered around the world, it looked like there might be no venues open to even show *Earwig and the Witch*.

However, when the project was unveiled by Toshio Suzuki in June 2020, it was announced that *Earwig* would screen not in cinemas but on television, with a date set for a festive premiere in late December. Later that month, it was also revealed that the film would have received a world premiere at the Cannes Film Festival, had the festival not been postponed due to the pandemic. He may have missed out on a glitzy red-carpet premiere on the French Riviera, but Goro had achieved the distinction of making Ghibli's first Japanese film to appear in Cannes' prestigious Official Selection.

But the question still stood: what would the world make of *Earwig and the Witch*, and Ghibli's new direction? After 35 years of distinctive hand-drawn animation, the film looked like a break from the established, beloved norm.

*Earwig* appeared on screens in the English-speaking world in 2021, first as a limited theatrical release in the USA in February from GKIDS, followed by a streaming premiere on HBO Max, and a cinema release in the UK from the new outfit Elysian Film Group, making it the first Ghibli film in decades not to be released by StudioCanal. It was also the first Ghibli film to receive a public, big-screen rollout in the West before it hit cinemas back home – which it finally did that April.

Reviews were among the most scathing ever written about a Ghibli film. Kristy Puchko of *Pajiba* described the film as feeling "like a cheap knock-off of Studio Ghibli", while Simon Abrams, writing for the website maintained in honour of Ghibli's great champion, Roger Ebert, called Earwig "a lumpy cover version of Hayao's greatest hits".

*Earwig and the Witch* is an undeniably daring experiment under the Ghibli name, but Goro Miyazaki found himself, once again, unfairly judged against the precedence of his father and his world-conquering films.

**Opposite:** A young, dark-haired girl, broom handle in hand, black cat by her side and curious about magic may seem like familiar Ghibli territory. But beware: the bratty Earwig is no Kiki.

*Earwig and the Witch* might just be Studio Ghibli's most experimental film. Read the script and you might ask why, because the story of a young witch and her cat, set against a rural European backdrop, sounds like another page from the classic Ghibli recipe book. But take one look at it and it's instantly clear: this isn't just a new film for Ghibli, it's a whole new dimension.

The studio's foray into 3D computer-generated animation makes for strange, almost uncanny, viewing. Backgrounds of blue skies, green hills and ocean horizons provide a foundation of relievingly recognizable imagery, but the characters that reside in this new world are far from comforting. Instead of the expressive, almost artistically tangible, work that one has come to expect, here the people seem to have been squeezed out of a plastics factory line. Their skin is too smooth, their expressions are robotic, and their hair has the solidity of a Lego figure's. In the moments when emotion must be translated, a mainstream 'anime' style is applied to Earwig and her fellow 3D residents, where eyes widen or tighten to extreme proportions and mouths envelop a whole face to scream. These cartoonish contortions might not sound too outlandish, but elsewhere in the film things are animated to such hyper-detail (including an admittedly incredible looking plate of fish and chips), that together they make for a clash of realities and an unnerving stylistic dissonance.

Under the surface level, which in this case is probably the best place to look, there are some interesting ideas bubbling away in the film's creative cauldron. The bulk of the story revolves around the bratty young orphan Earwig being adopted by a nefarious magical duo named Bella Yaga and The Mandrake. They promise her that they'll teach her how to brew magic spells, but in reality she's left scrubbing the pots. Here spells and potions come with a cookbook; we've seen before how magical a Ghibli kitchen can be, but here it really is. Earwig can follow instructions to create enchantments and in doing so learn her craft, democratizing magic and making it something attainable to all, providing they can put in the work. Although the story might initially seem like a companion to the magical adventure of *Kiki's Delivery Service*, philosophically this suggests more alignment to the lessons on hard work and creative practice found in the real world of *Whisper of the Heart*.

Earwig does finally get her magic, but then disappointingly she wields it like the brat she always was, the abrupt ending of the film slamming in before any lessons are actually learned. One can only hope that at Studio Ghibli that isn't the case and the lessons of this excursion into 3DCG have very much been absorbed. Although some may wish for this venture to have a similarly abrupt ending, the prospect of Studio Ghibli experimenting is and should always be exciting. Let's see them stir the magic cauldron, who knows what might come next, it could be delicious.

**Opposite:** The English-language release poster for *Earwig and the Witch*.

**Below:** Full marks as a wizard, zero marks as a foster father. Wizard, wannabe author and one-time rock band keyboardist The Mandrake, the second of Earwig's sinister foster parents.

# FURTHER READING AND WATCHING

For the production history and background information in this book, we are indebted to a number of writers, sources, documentaries and translated texts that are all listed below. We also drew from over a decade of personal research, including our own interviews with Isao Takahata, Toshio Suzuki, Gorō Miyazaki, Hiromasa Yonebayashi, Yoshiaki Nishimura, Kathleen Kennedy, Michaël Dudok de Wit, Mami Sunada and Steve Alpert.

Thanks, too, to StudioCanal, GKIDS and Elysian Films for press materials that were crucial to the process of piecing together the story of Studio Ghibli. Box office placements and statistics were taken from the Motion Picture Producers Association of Japan (Eiren.org), and every Studio Ghibli fan must acknowledge the invaluable work of *GhibliWiki* (Nausicaa.net) and *Buta Connection* (Buta-connection.net) for maintaining accessible and exhaustive online resources for all things Ghibli.

## BOOKS

Alpert, Steve, *Sharing a House with the Never-Ending Man* (Berkeley, Stone Bridge Press, 2020)

Clements, Jonathan & McCarthy, Helen, *The Anime Encyclopedia, 3rd Revised Edition: A Century of Japanese Animation* (Berkeley, Stone Bridge Press, 2015)

Denison, Rayna (ed.), *Princess Mononoke: Understanding Studio Ghibli's Monster Princess* (London, Bloomsbury Academic, 2018)

Dudok de Wit, Alex, *BFI Film Classics: Grave of the Fireflies* (London, Bloomsbury Publishing, 2021)

Hara, Kunio, *33¹/₃ Japan: My Neighbor Totoro Soundtrack* (London, Bloomsbury Academic, 2020)

Martin, Daniel, *BFI Film Classics: Kiki's Delivery Service* (London, Bloomsbury Publishing, 2022)

McCarthy, Helen, *Hayao Miyazaki: Master of Japanese Animation* (Berkeley, Stone Bridge Press, 1999)

Miyazaki, Hayao, *Starting Point: 1979–1996* (San Francisco, Viz Media, 2009)

Miyazaki, Hayao, *Turning Point: 1997–2008* (San Francisco, Viz Media, 2014)

Napier, Susan, *Miyazakiworld: A Life in Art* (London, Yale University Press, 2018)

Odell, Colin & Le Blanc, Michelle, *Studio Ghibli: The Films of Hayao Miyazaki and Isao Takahata* (Harpenden, Hertfordshire, Kamera Books, 2009)

Osmond, Andrew, *BFI Film Classics: Spirited Away* (London, Bloomsbury Publishing, 2008)

Ruzic, Andrijana, *Michaël Dudok de Wit: A Life in Animation* (Boca Raton, Florida, CRC Press, 2020)

Suzuki, Toshio, *Mixing Work and Pleasure: My Life at Studio Ghibli* (Tokyo, Japan Publishing Industry Foundation for Culture, 2018)

Wynne Jones, Diana, *Howl's Moving Castle* (London, HarperCollins Children's Books, 2009)

## DOCUMENTARIES

*10 Years with Hayao Miyazaki* (dir. Kaku Arakawa, 2019)

*Isao Takahata and His Tale of the Princess Kaguya* (dirs. Akira Miki, Hidekazu Sato, 2014)

*The Kingdom of Dreams and Madness* ( dir. Mami Sunada, 2013)

*Never-Ending Man: Hayao Miyazaki* (dir. Kaku Arakawa, 2016)

## ARTICLES, INTERVIEWS AND BLOGS

'Hayao Miyazaki Interview: Reasons why I don't make Slapstick Action Films now', *Comic Box*, October 1989. Translated by Atsushi Fukumoto, Sheng-Te Tsao and Steven Feldman.
http://www.nausicaa.net/miyazaki/interviews/slapstick.html#fn2

'In This Corner of The World: An Exclusive Interview with Director Sunao Katabuchi", WaveMotionCannon.com, August 15, 2017.
https://wavemotioncannon.com/2017/08/15/in-this-corner-of-the-world-an-exclusive-interview-with-director-sunao-katabuchi/

'Interview: Miyazaki on *Sen to Chihiro no Kamikakushi*', *Animage*, May 2001. Translated by Ryoko Toyama.
http://www.nausicaa.net/miyazaki/interviews/sen.html

'Remembering Takahata Isao, 1935–2018', *Sight & Sound*, May 14, 2018.
https://www2.bfi.org.uk/news-opinion/sight-soundmagazine/comment/obituaries/remembering-takahata-isao-1935-2018

'Special Interview: Suzuki Toshio, Producer and Chairman, Studio Ghibli – Miyazaki Hayao and Takahata Isao Serving as the driver for two geniuses', Japan Policy Forum, October 11, 2013
https://www.japanpolicyforum.jp/culture/pt20131011203452.html

Abrams, Simon, ,Earwig and the Witch', RogerEbert.com,
February 3 2021. https://www.rogerebert.com/reviews/earwig-and-the-witch-film-review-2021

Brooks, Xan, 'A god among animators', the *Guardian*, September 14, 2005.
https://www.theguardian.com/film/2005/sep/14/japan.awardsandprizes

Capone, 'Comic-Con '09: Capone Chats With The Mighty Hayao Miyazaki about his Latest, PONYO!!', *Ain't It Cool News*, August 3, 2009.
http://legacy.aintitcool.com/node/41918

Ebert, Roger, 'My Neighbor Totoro', RogerEbert.com, December 23, 2001.
https://www.rogerebert.com/reviews/great-movie-my-neighbor-totoro-1993

Hikawa, Ryūsuke, 'The Classic Storytelling of Anime Director Hosoda Mamoru', *Nippon.com*, November 17, 2016.
https://www.nippon.com/en/views/b06801/the-classic-storytelling-of-anime-director-hosoda-mamoru.html#

Le Guin, Ursula K., 'A First Response to "Gedo Senki," the Earthsea film made by Goro Miyazaki for Studio Ghibli', *UrsulaKLeGuin.com*
https://www.ursulakleguin.com/gedo-senki-1

McCarthy, Helen, 'The House That Hayao Built', *Manga Max*, 1999.

Puchko, Kristy, 'Now on HBO Max: 'Earwig and the Witch' Is The Latest From Studio Ghibli', Pajiba, February 5, 2021. https://www.pajiba.com/film_reviews/now-on-hbo-max-earwig-and-the-witch-is-the-latest-from-studio-ghibli.php

Stimson, Eric, 'Ghibli's Suzuki Reveals Circumstances Behind Laputa's Production', Anime News Network, September 25, 2014.
https://www.animenewsnetwork.com/interest/2014-09-24/ghibli-suzuki-reveals-circumstances-behind-laputa-production/.79131

"New Tweets per second record, and how!" blog.twitter.com, August 16, 2013. https://blog.twitter.com/engineering/en_us/a/2013/new-tweets-per-second-record-and-how.html

Roger Ebert, 'Grave of the Fireflies', RogerEbert.com, March 19, 2000
- https://www.rogerebert.com/reviews/great-movie-grave-of-the-fireflies-1988

# PHOTO CREDITS

The publishers would like to thank the following sources for their kind permission to reproduce the pictures in this book.

5 Jeremy Sutton-Hibbert / Alamy Stock Photo; 6 coward_lion / Alamy Stock Photo; 7 (Left) 2001 Studio Ghibli - NDDTM; (Centre) AUTHORS; (Right) Everett Collection Inc / Alamy Stock Photo; 8 Gonzalo Azumendi / Alamy Stock Photo; 9 Jérémie Souteyrat; 10-11 Jérémie Souteyrat; 12 Spencer Weiner/Los Angeles Times via Getty; 13 Newscom/Alamy Live News; 14 1984 Studio Ghibli – H; 15 1984 Studio Ghibli – H; 16 (Top) Newscom / Alamy Stock Photo; 17 HAKUHODO/ NIBARIKI/TOKUMA; 18 (Top and bottom) 1984 Studio Ghibli – H; 19 Everett Collection, Inc. / Alamy Stock Photo; 20 1984 Studio Ghibli – H; 21 1984 Studio Ghibli – H; 22 AF archive / Alamy Stock Photo; 23 1986 Studio Ghibli; 24 1986 Studio Ghibli; 25 STUDIO GHIBLI / Album; 26 1986 Studio Ghibli; 27 Photo 12 / Alamy Stock Photo; 28 1986 Studio Ghibli; 29 1986 Studio Ghibli; 30 Photo 12 / Alamy Stock Photo; 31 1988 Studio Ghibli; 32 (Top and Bottom) 1988 Studio Ghibli; 33 Laurent KOFFEL/ Gamma-Rapho; 34-35 Photo 12 / Alamy Stock Photo; 36 AUTHORS; 37 AF archive / Alamy Stock Photo; 38 1988 Studio Ghibli; 39 1988 Studio Ghibli; 40 1988 Studio Ghibli; 41 Gkids /Courtesy Everett Collection; 42 1988 Studio Ghibli; 43 Studio Ghibli/courtesy Everett Collection; 44 1988 Studio Ghibli; 45 1988 Studio Ghibli; 46 The Asahi Shimbun via Getty Images; 47 1988 Studio Ghibli; 48 AF archive / Alamy Stock Photo; 50 1988 Studio Ghibli – N; 51 1988 Studio Ghibli – N; 52 Jérémie Souteyrat; 53 Photo 12 / Alamy Stock Photo; 54-55 1988 Studio Ghibli – N; 57 STUDIO GHIBLI / Album; 58 1991 Hotaru Okamoto - Yuko Tone - Studio Ghibli – NH; 59 1991 Hotaru Okamoto - Yuko Tone - Studio Ghibli – NH; 60 Photo 12 / Alamy Stock Photo; 61 1991 Hotaru Okamoto - Yuko Tone - Studio Ghibli – NH; 62 AUTHORS; 63 1991 Hotaru Okamoto - Yuko Tone - Studio Ghibli – NH; 64 1992 Studio Ghibli – NN; 65 1992 Studio Ghibli – NN; 66 Jérémie Souteyrat; 67 1992 Studio Ghibli – NN; 68 1992 Studio Ghibli – NN; 69 Photo 12 / Alamy Stock Photo; 70 1992 Studio Ghibli – NN; 71 1992 Studio Ghibli – NN; 72 1993 Saeko Himuro - Studio Ghibli – N; 73 1993 Saeko Himuro - Studio Ghibli – N; 74 1993 Saeko Himuro - Studio Ghibli – N; 75 Everett Collection Inc / Alamy Stock Photo; 76 1994 Hatake Jimusho - Studio Ghibli – NH; 77 1994 Hatake Jimusho - Studio Ghibli - NH; 78 Buena Vista Home Video/Courtesy Everett Collection; 79 1994 Hatake Jimusho - Studio Ghibli – NH; 80 1994 Hatake Jimusho - Studio Ghibli – NH; 81 1994 Hatake Jimusho - Studio Ghibli – NH; 82 1995 Aoi Hiiragi / Shueisha - Studio Ghibli – NH; 83 1995 Aoi Hiiragi / Shueisha - Studio Ghibli – NH; 84 1995 Aoi Hiiragi / Shueisha - Studio Ghibli – NH; 85 Gkids / courtesy Everett Collection; 86-87 1995 Aoi Hiiragi / Shueisha - Studio Ghibli – NH; 88 Photo 12 / Alamy Stock Photo; 89 1995 Aoi Hiiragi / Shueisha - Studio Ghibli – NH; 90 1995 Aoi Hiiragi / Shueisha - Studio Ghibli – NH; 91 (Top) AUTHORS; (Bottom) 1995 Aoi Hiiragi / Shueisha - Studio Ghibli - NH; 92 1997 Studio Ghibli – ND; 93 1997 Studio Ghibli – ND; 94 1997 Studio Ghibli – ND; 95 Album / Alamy Stock Photo; 96 The Asahi Shimbun via Getty Images; 97 1997 Studio Ghibli – ND; 98 1997 Studio Ghibli – ND; 99 Globe Photos/ZUMAPRESS.com; 100 1997 Studio Ghibli – ND; 101 1997 Studio Ghibli – ND; 102 1999 Hisaichi Ishii - Hatake Jimusho - Studio Ghibli – NHD; 103 1999 Hisaichi Ishii - Hatake Jimusho - Studio Ghibli – NHD; 104 Photo 12 / Alamy Stock Photo; 105 1999 Hisaichi Ishii - Hatake Jimusho - Studio Ghibli – NHD; 106 1999 Hisaichi Ishii - Hatake Jimusho - Studio Ghibli – NHD; 107 (Top and Bottom) 1999 Hisaichi Ishii - Hatake Jimusho - Studio Ghibli – NHD; 108 2001 Studio Ghibli – NDDTM; 109 2001 Studio Ghibli – NDDTM; 110 (Top) Jennifer Abe / Alamy Stock Photo; (Bottom) AF archive / Alamy Stock Photo; 111 Everett Collection Inc / Alamy Stock Photo; 112-113 2001 Studio

Ghibli – NDDTM; 114 The Asahi Shimbun via Getty Images; 115 Entertainment Pictures / Alamy Stock Photo; 116 2001 Studio Ghibli – NDDTM; 117 Jérémie Souteyrat; 118 2002 Nekonote-Do - Studio Ghibli – NDHMT; 119 2002 Nekonote-Do - Studio Ghibli – NDHMT; 120 2002 Nekonote-Do - Studio Ghibli – NDHMT; 121 Photo 12 / Alamy Stock Photo; 122 2004 Studio Ghibli – NDDMT; 123 2004 Studio Ghibli – NDDMT; 124 Photo 12 / Alamy Stock Photo; 125 2004 Studio Ghibli – NDDMT; 126 (Top) REUTERS / Alamy Stock Photo; (Bottom) Francis Specker / Alamy Stock Photo; 127 2004 Studio Ghibli – NDDMT; 128 (Top) and (Bottom) 2004 Studio Ghibli – NDDMT; 130 2006 Studio Ghibli – NDHDMT; 131 2006 Studio Ghibli – NDHDMT; 132 TORU YAMANAKA/AFP; 133 Photo 12 / Alamy Stock Photo; 134 2006 Studio Ghibli – NDHDMT; 135 2006 Studio Ghibli – NDHDMT; 136 2008 Studio Ghibli – NDHDMT; 137 2008 Studio Ghibli – NDHDMT; 138-139 2008 Studio Ghibli – NDHDMT; 140 2008 Studio Ghibli – NDHDMT; 141 (Top) UPI / Alamy Stock Photo; (Bottom) Horizon Images/Motion / Alamy Stock Photo; 143 Everett Collection Inc / Alamy Stock Photo; 144 2010 Studio Ghibli - NDHDMTW; 145 2010 Studio Ghibli – NDHDMTW; 146 STUDIO GHIBLI / Album; 147 2010 Studio Ghibli – NDHDMTW; 148 2010 Studio Ghibli – NDHDMTW; 149 2010 Studio Ghibli – NDHDMTW; 150 Photo 12 / Alamy Stock Photo; 151 2011 Chizuru Takahashi - Tetsuro Sayama - Studio Ghibli – NDHDMT; 152 2011 Chizuru Takahashi - Tetsuro Sayama - Studio Ghibli – NDHDMT; 153 Photo 12 / Alamy Stock Photo; 154 Photo 12 / Alamy Stock Photo; 155 REUTERS / Alamy Stock Photo; 156 Allstar Picture Library Ltd. / Alamy Stock Photo; 157 Collection Christophel  Studio Ghibli / DR; 158 2013 Studio Ghibli – NDHDMTK; 159 Everett Collection Inc / Alamy Stock Photo; 160-161 2013 Studio Ghibli – NDHDMTK; 162 Everett Collection Inc / Alamy Stock Photo; 163 2013 Studio Ghibli – NDHDMTK; 164 2013 Studio Ghibli - NDHDMTK; 165 2013 Studio Ghibli – NDHDMTK; 166 2013 Studio Ghibli – NDHDMTK; 167 2013 Hatake Jimusho - Studio Ghibli – NDHDMTK; 168 (Top and Bottom) 2013 Hatake Jimusho - Studio Ghibli – NDHDMTK; 169 Newscom / Alamy Stock Photo; 170-171 2013 Hatake Jimusho - Studio Ghibli – NDHDMTK; 172 REUTERS/Jonathan Alcorn; 173 STUDIO GHIBLI / Album; 174 2013 Hatake Jimusho - Studio Ghibli – NDHDMTK; 175 2013 Hatake Jimusho - Studio Ghibli – NDHDMTK; 176 2014 Studio Ghibli - NDHDMTK; 177 2014 Studio Ghibli – NDHDMTK; 178 Jérémie Souteyrat; 179 2014 Studio Ghibli – NDHDMTK; 180 Photo 12 / Alamy Stock Photo; 181 Jérémie Souteyrat; 182 2016 Studio Ghibli; 183 2016 Studio Ghibli; 184 2016 Studio Ghibli; 185 Everett Collection Inc / Alamy Stock Photo; 186 "2020 NHK, NEP, Studio Ghibli"; 188 "2020 NHK, NEP, Studio Ghibli"; 189 "2020 NHK, NEP, Studio Ghibli".

Every effort has been made to acknowledge correctly and contact the source and/or copyright holder of each picture and Welbeck Non-Fiction Limited apologizes for any unintentional errors or omissions, which will be corrected in future editions of this book.

# INDEX